EVOLUTIONARY THINKING

CAC Publishing
Center for Action and Contemplation
cac.org

"*Oneing*" is an old English word that was used by Lady Julian of Norwich (1342–1416) to describe the encounter between God and the soul. The Center for Action and Contemplation proudly borrows the word to express the divine unity that stands behind all of the divisions, dichotomies, and dualisms in the world. We pray and publish with Jesus' words, "that all may be one" (John 17:21).

EDITOR:
Vanessa Guerin

PUBLISHER:
The Center for Action and Contemplation

ADVISORY BOARD:
David Benner
James Danaher
Ilia Delio, OSF
Sheryl Fullerton
Stephen Gaertner, OPraem
Ruth Patterson

Design and Composition by Nelson Kane Design

Tree ring prints on cover and throughout interior by Linne Hutto, http://timberwoodengoods.com

© 2016 Center for Action and Contemplation.
All rights reserved.

Oneing
VOLUME 4 NO. 2

RICHARD ROHR
Introduction   13

VIRGINIA WEIR
Nada Mas   15

STEVE MILLS
Negative Space   17

BRITTIAN BULLOCK and MIKE MORRELL
Evolving Wild:
Glimpses of the Garden City   23

MICHAEL DOWD
Evidential Medicine for Our Collective Soul   35

TERESA PASQUALE MATEUS
Mystic Love, Unbound:
A Reclaimed, Reframed, and Evolving
Love Story between God and the World   45

TASHA WAHL
The Evolution of Love   53

MARIO SIKORA
Instinctual Biases:
How Understanding Our Evolutionary Past
Can Help Free Us from Our Cage   59

BRIE STONER
Joining the Dance of Evolution:
Restoring the Power of Belief and Creativity
in the Midst of Conflict and Crisis   67

SALLY K. SEVERINO
   Reflections on the Life of Pope Francis:
      The Formation of an Evolutionary Thinker   75

ALISON KIRKPATRICK
   Raising a Feminist Son   83

RAY LEONARDINI
   What No Bars Can Hold   89

JONATHON STALLS
   What Really Frightens Us?   97

MICKY SCOTTBEY JONES
   [R]evolutionary Salvation   105

RICHARD ROHR
   Evolution Is another Name for Growth   111

NOTES   117

EDITOR'S NOTE

Evolutionary thinking is actually contemplative thinking because it leaves the full field of the future in God's hands and agrees to humbly hold the present with what it only tentatively knows for sure.

—Richard Rohr

IN HER INTERVIEW with Sam Mowe, "The Unfolding Story of the Universe," Mary Evelyn Tucker says something similar to the quote above: "When we look at pictures from the Hubble telescope, that's contemplation. You get the feeling of, 'Wow, was I birthed out of these systems?' The stars really are our ancestors—literally and metaphorically." But she also reminds us that "there is the simultaneous awareness in our time of the beauty of evolution and...of extinction and this destruction we're causing on the planet." Yet, she remains hopeful.

This hopefulness is exemplified in "The Evolution of Love," by Tasha Wahl, who addresses the theme of this edition of *Oneing* on a more personal level—the evolution of her marriage. She writes, "I have been married for twenty-two years to multiple men—dozens, maybe even hundreds. They are all named Erik, but they are as unique as the stars in the sky." She candidly shares how she had to let go of "the man [she] married" in order to evolve into the person she is today. She bears witness to the hope that is possible in a marriage between two developing, creative individuals: "My story, and all the men in it, is a far more interesting story than the one I thought I wanted, because this story is a living, changing evolution of love."

Jonathon Stalls writes about a different kind of relationship in "What Really Frightens Us?" After walking the Camino de Santiago in Spain, he takes a three-thousand-mile journey across the United States—a journey of "profound growth, connection, simplicity, and authentic transformation, found in moving the way we're built to move—by foot." He writes in a lovely, poetic way about the many people he encounters along the way and his gratitude for the ways in which they welcome him into their lives: "My steps were anchored in hospitality offered at the homes and dinner tables of 120 'strangers' from rural, suburban, and urban communities, which included families, partnerships, single mothers, college students, commune dwellers, public officials, professional musicians, police officers—all from different political, religious, racial, sexual, and economic stock." A solitary journey that began with intentional presence to the experience of walking evolved into an expedition of hope, grounded in a renewed and expanded faith in that family of strangers.

While the incarcerated may not have the freedom to trek long distances in the open air, the opportunity to experience freedom presents itself to them in another way. In "What No Bars Can Hold," Ray Leonardini reflects on the evolution of the prisoners with whom he works at Folsom Prison. "When I bring up topics for discussion, we create a space that allows for empowerment, particularly in the exchange of personal feelings and sharing of long-held wounds." This would not be possible if he had not introduced the prisoners to the practice of Centering Prayer. Through Centering Prayer, prisoners have learned the practice of presence—to the Divine and to one another. This practice has proved to be a critical coping tool, especially in times when they find themselves feeling triggered. It has allowed them to remember to pause before reacting and to take the opportunity to reflect back in calm, strong, yet sensitive ways.

I first read a condensed version of Alison Kirkpatrick's article, "Raising a Feminist Son," long before I began to consider how an edition on "Evolutionary Thinking" might look. Her article became the catalyst for considering the many ways we need to look at evolution—not only in the grand, universal scheme, but in the very way any evolutionary process is brought into fruition—from its earliest years.

I would encourage you, dear reader, to study each and every piece in this very full edition of *Oneing* as if the entire edition was a single article. Hopefully, you will be inspired to look through a newly polished lens and realize that we are all participating in the beauty of our own evolutionary process—as we leave the "full field of the future in God's hands and [agree] to humbly hold the present with what it only tentatively knows for sure."

Vanessa Guerin,
Editor

CONTRIBUTORS

RICHARD ROHR is a Franciscan priest of the New Mexico Province and the Founding Director of the Center for Action and Contemplation (CAC) in Albuquerque, New Mexico. An internationally recognized author and spiritual leader, Fr. Richard teaches primarily on incarnational mysticism, non-dual consciousness, and contemplation, with a particular emphasis on how these affect the social justice issues of our time. Along with many recorded conferences, he is the author of numerous books, including the newly published *The Divine Dance: The Trinity and Your Transformation* (with Mike Morrell) and *A Spring Within Us: A Book of Daily Meditations*. To learn more about Fr. Richard Rohr and the CAC, visit https://cac.org/richard-rohr/richard-rohr-ofm/.

VIRGINIA WEIR, an alumna of the Center for Action and Contemplation's Living School for Action and Contemplation, works as a fundraiser for a large social service agency in Bridgeport, Connecticut. She enjoys writing and received her MFA in fiction from Warren Wilson College in Swannanoa, North Carolina. A poet, Virginia's contribution to this edition of *Oneing*, "Nada Mas," is taken from a chapbook titled *Course Rind, Sweet Fruit*, created as part of her experience at the Living School. The mother of two grown children, Virginia Weir may be contacted at vlweir1@gmail.com.

STEVE MILLS, an aerospace scientist, specializes in calibrating the NASA and NOAA satellites, the instruments used to measure the Earth's weather, climate, and environment. He has thirty-five years' experience in the aerospace industry, covering all aspects of optical sensor development from concept definition, system design, algorithm development, integration/test, launch, and in-orbit operation through satellite end-of-life. He has written numerous technical papers and is the owner of Renaissance Man Engineering, which provides tools and training so that educators and researchers can more easily access and understand satellite data. In addition to his scientific work, he paints and writes music, prose, and poetry. He lives in Glendale, California. To learn more about Steve Mills and his company, Renaissance Man Engineering, visit http://renmaneng.com/.

BRITTIAN BULLOCK, MA, MHP, is a clinical therapist utilizing contemplative-based counseling to work with a wide range of clients, from the chronically suicidal to those searching for spiritual direction. He also teaches graduate courses that focus on theories of human development, ecology, and the impact of civilization on mental health. Brittian lived for over a decade in a neo-monastic community, drawing on the rich tradition of both Catholic and Protestant mystics. He is a writer, speaker, and teacher interested in primal spirituality and heartful living. Brittian, his wife, and their four children live near Portland, Oregon. To learn more about Brittian Bullock's ongoing meditations on trauma, wholeness, therapy, and a life well-lived, visit http://BrittianBullock.com/.

MIKE MORRELL is Communications Director for the Integral Theology think tank Presence International. He is co-founder of The Buzz Seminar and a founding organizer of the Wild Goose Festival. Mike curates contemplative and community experiences via Relational Yoga, the ManKind Project, (H) Opp, and Authentic North Carolina, taking joy in holding space for the extraordinary transformation that can take place at the intersection of anticipation, imagination, and radical acceptance. Mike is also an avid writer, publishing consultant, author coach, futurist, and curator of the book-reviewing community at TheSpeakeasy.info. He lives with his wife and two daughters in North Carolina. To learn more about Mike Morrell's ongoing exploration of Spirit, Culture, and Permaculture, and receive free exclusive updates, visit http://MikeMorrell.org/.

THE REV. MICHAEL DOWD, MDiv, is a bestselling evolutionary eco-theologian and pro-future evangelist whose work has been featured in *The New York Times, Los Angeles Times, Wall Street Journal, Washington Post, Newsweek, Discover,* and on national television. His 2009 book, *Thank God for Evolution,* was endorsed by six Nobel Prize-winning scientists, noted skeptics, and religious leaders across the spectrum. Michael and his wife—science writer, evolutionary educator, and fellow climate activist Connie Barlow—have addressed more than two thousand groups throughout the U.S. and Canada since 2002. Michael has also delivered two TEDx talks, a program at the United Nations, and conducted two acclaimed online conversation series: "The Advent of Evolutionary Christianity" and "The Future Is Calling Us to Greatness." To learn more about Michael Dowd's pro-science ministry, visit StandingfortheFuture.org, http://TheGreatStory.org, or http://MichaelDowd.org/.

TERESA PASQUALE MATEUS is a writer, speaker, trauma therapist, and yoga and contemplative practice teacher based in Chicago, Illinois. She holds a BA from Montclair State University in English and Women Studies, an MSW from New York University in Clinical Social Work, and is an alumna of the Center for Action and Contemplation's Living School for Action and Contemplation. Teresa is author of two books on trauma, spirituality, and healing: *Sacred Wounds: A Path to Healing from Spiritual Trauma* and *Mending Broken: A Personal Journey Through the Stages of Trauma and Recovery*. She is currently working on projects related to the integration of contemplation and action—one specifically focused on people of color and their experience in the contemplative Christian context. To learn more about Teresa Pasquale Mateus, visit http://www.teresabpasquale.com or contact her directly at tbpasquale@gmail.com.

TASHA WAHL, wife, mother, daughter, friend, artist, writer, photographer, runner, philanthropist, seeker, co-creator with the incarnate Christ, is the founder of Butterfly Effect—an underground movement "redefining philanthropy one butterfly at a time" by providing individuals the opportunity to give to a cause close to their hearts. Harnessing the power of social media, Butterfly Effect creates a ripple effect of contagious generosity, recognizing that we can "be the change we wish to see in the world" by facilitating small acts of kindness, encouraging generosity, and promoting creativity. An alumna of the Center for Action and Contemplation's Living School for Action and Contemplation, Tasha is Executive Director for The Wahl Group, Inc., http://www.theartofvision.com. To learn more about Tasha Wahl, visit http://www.butterflyeffectbethechange.com.

MARIO SIKORA, an internationally recognized speaker and author, is president and executive coach of Awareness to Action International. A leadership consultant for nearly twenty years, he has advised executives in large organizations across the globe, including Motorola, TE Connectivity, Dow Chemical Company, Panasonic, Arris, Rovi Corporation, and Johnson & Johnson. Together with Robert Tallon, Mario is co-author of *Awareness to Action: The Enneagram, Emotional Intelligence, and Change*. He has written numerous articles on personality styles and leadership, performance improvement, and teambuilding. Mario's writings have been translated into Italian, Spanish, French, Turkish, Portuguese, Arabic, Russian, Korean, and Danish. To learn more about Mario Sikora, visit http://www.awarenesstoaction.com. To learn more about the instinctual biases, visit http://www.EnneagramVideos.com.

Gabrielle "Brie" Stoner is a musician, writer, student, and 2015 alumna of the Center for Action and Contemplation's Living School for Action and Contemplation. Her music, which has been featured in national and international television broadcasting, includes the production and composition of the soundtracks for the NOOMA film series with Rob Bell. Brie has published blogs for The Contemplative Society, Northeast Wisdom, and The Wisdom Way of Knowing websites, and contributed to an anthology dedicated to the work of Teilhard de Chardin and Beatrice Bruteau, edited by Ilia Delio, OSF: *Personal Transformation and a New Creation: The Spiritual Revolution of Beatrice Bruteau*. Brie currently serves as the content coordinator for The Omega Center, an online education forum initiative of Ilia Delio, and as a research assistant to Cynthia Bourgeault. Mother of two sons, she is currently enrolled in the Chicago Theological Seminary's graduate program, continuing her studies on Teilhard de Chardin, about whose work she regularly writes on her own blog: http://www.becomingultrahuman.com.

Sally K. Severino, MD, is an author, speaker, and Professor Emeritus of Psychiatry at the University of New Mexico Health Sciences Center. Grounded in the Christian contemplative tradition, she is a Felician Associate of the Assumption of the Blessed Virgin Mary Convent. Her book with Dr. Nancy Morrison, *Sacred Desire: Growing in Compassionate Living*, won the 2014 Eric Hoffer award in the category of Legacy Nonfiction. To learn more about Sally K. Severino, visit http://www.neurospirit.net.

Alison Kirkpatrick is an educator, freelance writer, blogger, speaker, and retreat leader. As an alumna of The Living School for Action and Contemplation, she is deeply committed to integrating her contemplative practices and studies into her everyday life as a wife, mother, and community builder. You can find more of her reflections on the intersection of spirituality and current events, faith, and family life on her blog, #Signs of Love, at http://www.alisonkirkpatrick.com.

Ray Leonardini practiced law for nearly thirty years. After retirement, he turned toward his foremost area of interest: the Christian spiritual journey. For the last nine years, as a volunteer chaplain, he has led meditation groups and taught contemplative prayer and the spiritual journey at Folsom State Prison and other prisons in Northern California. He is the Director of Prison Contemplative Fellowship, a nonprofit organization that sends books and prayer materials directly to prisoners, and works with prison chaplains and volunteers to facilitate the startup of centering prayer groups. He is the author of *Finding God Within: Contemplative Prayer for Prisoners*, a handbook written specifically for prisoners which has been sent to more than seven hundred prisoners throughout the country and is used for centering prayer groups in over one hundred prisons and jails. The Spanish translation of the book is used in Guatemalan prisons. His newest book, *Going Inside: Learning to Teach Contemplative Prayer to the Imprisoned*, was released in September, 2016. You can reach Ray Leonardini at office@USPCF.org.

JONATHON STALLS founded Walk2Connect in 2012, shortly after completing the Camino de Santiago in Spain and an eight-and-a-half-month, three-thousand-mile walk across the United States in 2010. He has extensive experience in community outreach, partnership development, communications, social enterprise, and movement building around issues related to walking for whole health and walkable community education. Jonathon continues to walk thousands of miles, guiding hundreds of personal, social, communal, and spiritual walking experiences with individuals, couples, groups, and organizations throughout the country. In 2013, Jonathon was featured in a *New York Times* article titled "Walking the Land As a Spiritual Quest" and a TEDx talk titled "Life at 3MPH." He is a student of the Center for Action and Contemplation's Living School for Action and Contemplation. To learn more about Jonathon Stalls and Walk2Connect, visit http://walk2connect.com/.

MICKY SCOTTBEY JONES is a perpetual learner, "justice doula," consultant, facilitator, mama/sister/friend, nonviolence practitioner, and contemplative activist. After more than ten years as a mother-baby specialist, trainer, and author, she shifted back to her earlier interests in theology and community development. She is a member of the co-learning community of North American Institute of Indigenous Theological Studies and graduated with a Masters of Arts in Intercultural Studies. Micky facilitates conferences, trainings, and online conversations while exploring a variety of topics including self-care in community (healing justice), intersectionality, faith-rooted activism, revolutionary friendship, race and justice, and theology from the margins. She loves to curate contemplative and dialogic spaces and activities. Named one of the "Black Christian Leaders Changing the World" in *The Huffington Post* in 2015, Micky is a core member of the Faith Matters Network and consults with a variety of projects and organizations as opportunities arise. She is currently serving as an Associate Fellow for Racial Justice with Evangelicals for Social Action and serves her local community as an organizer with the Nashville Children's Defense Fund Office. To learn more about Micky ScottBey Jones, visit http://www.mickyscottbeyjones.com/.

INTRODUCTION

The whole creation is eagerly waiting for the full revelation of the children of God.... From the beginning until now, the entire creation, as we know, has been groaning in one great act of giving birth.

(See Romans 8:19–22)

IN THIS CLASSIC QUOTE, St. Paul does not actively teach what we now call evolution; rather, I think he fully assumes it when he says, parenthetically, "as we know."

It has always seemed completely strange to me that there should be any resistance whatsoever to evolution or evolutionary thinking in Christian theology or practice. Instead, Christians should have been the first in line to recognize and cooperate with such a dynamic notion of God. But maybe many do not enjoy such a relational God—with all that that implies—and have just met a "substance" they call God. A static notion of God makes everything else static too, including our very notions of spirituality, history, and religion.

Our rich understanding of the Trinity; the Indwelling Holy Spirit; the Mystery of Divine Incarnation; the notion of salvation revealed in the Judeo-Christian Scriptures—precisely in history itself; the self-evident witness of both human growth and historical unfolding; plus the formation of many developmental schemas, beginning with the desert period and continuing on through the Christian mystics—too many to count—all make it hard to imagine that so many still have a very static notion of God's being and divine action in the world. We still largely surrendered to a "pagan" and cyclical notion of time and, to make it worse, believed it was all leading up to Armageddon and Apocalypse—despite what we said about the resurrection. Even resurrection was understood as a static, one-time anomaly concerning only Jesus; few saw it as a portent and promise for us too (see 1 Corinthians

15:20–25), and fewer still recognized its relevance for the whole of creation, as Paul sees it in the quote above.

I can only assume that this reflects a very limited inner experience of God, which is always and predictably developmental and unfolding—never static. Anyone with an inner life of prayer and a sense of soul knows this to be true. Anybody who has paid any attention to their inner life or read any history books surely recognizes that life and love are always cumulative, growing, and going somewhere that is *always new and always more*. Perhaps it is this newness or moreness of which we are afraid. For some reason, we think that admitting such love dynamism and, in fact, cooperating with it (see Romans 8:28), is going to compromise our eternal, unchanging notion of God. Just the clearly evolving notion of "The Lord," and many other iterations in the Hebrew Scriptures, morphing into the Christian notion of Jesus and building up to the utterly relational and totally interactive doctrine of the Trinity, make a dynamic understanding of God not only rather obvious but also necessary—and even exciting.

If our God is both *incarnate and implanted*, both Christ and Holy Spirit, then an unfolding inner dynamism in all creation is not only certain, but also moving in a positive direction, and with a divine goal that is always beyond us. If not, we would have to question the very efficacy, salvation, hope, and victory that the Christian Gospel so generously promises. The strong death wishes, suicide bombing phenomenon, and high amount of mental aberration we experience in our world today is surely, in part, a result of our major failure to provide Western civilization with a positive and hopeful understanding of our own "good news." Foundational hope *demands* a foundational belief in a world that is still and always unfolding. Personally, I have found that it is almost impossible to heal individuals, over the long haul, if the whole cosmic arc is not also a trajectory toward the good.

As "children of the resurrection" (see Luke 20:36), we are both burdened and brightened by a cosmic and irrepressible hope—and we can never fully live up to it. We are both burdened and brightened with the gift of an optimism whose headwaters are neither rational, scientific, nor even provable to those who do not have it. Yet it ticks away from a deep place within us.

Richard Rohr

Nada Mas

Only love.
Only the holder the flag fits into,
and wind. No flag.
           —Rumi

Nada mas,
just this—
nothing more.
The flagline clangs flagless
against its pole.
The stubborn fly bangs its buzzing head
against the door.

Plain old
same old same-old,
nothing more.
What they said
would come to pass—
what rushes faster
and does not last—
has come,
and passed

Still, it's a kind of surprise.
this nothing,

this just-this,
this bent, almost broken bough
without forward or backward,
without hope, or fear
that clacks in the hot breeze and brushes
your shoulder as you pass—
gently, lightly, as if to say
Really, what more was it
you wanted?
To enjoy the something all the more
knowing it's nothing
is freedom

Relent.
Let go of your clinging,
your clanging and banging
No more looking over your shoulder to see
who is seeing
Soon enough, no more shoulder
to look over—

—Virginia Weir[1]

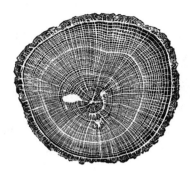

Negative Space

By *Steve Mills*

I FIRST ENCOUNTERED the term "negative space" while taking painting lessons. Negative space describes the empty space around or between things; for example, the space between a cup handle and the cup. Artists are taught to pay attention to the shape of the negative space because it can be as important as the solid objects are to the composition of the entire work.

As a scientist, I consider what it means to pay as much attention to what we don't see as to what we do. It seems that, throughout history, we humans have understood our world in terms of positive and negative space. There is the "positive space" of science—our understanding of the physical world, with its visible, immense power and movement. Even in ancient times, we had a rudimentary understanding of how the world works: the sun rises in the east and sets in the west; it is cold in the winter and warm in the summer (in the northern hemisphere, at least).

But there is also the negative space, the part of the world that we do not understand. We humans have assigned that negative space to the divine. When we could not see what moves the wind, we created a wind god. We could not reach the stars, so we made them the homes of our gods. We created these gods in the image of ourselves, but with added powers. They were really much like our comic-book superheroes, and we populated our pantheon with enough superhero gods and goddesses to fill all the negative space created by our limited understanding.

But when artists draw and paint the negative space, we do not imagine it as something else. We are taught to see it for what it is—the shape of something that we do not see. The problem with the superhero gods is that they were simply human imaginings, generated to fill that space. As an aid to the imagination, we made for ourselves images of our gods to reinforce our belief in their incredible powers.

But a different way was revealed to the ancient Hebrews. They rejected the pantheon of superheroes and replaced it with one God—and this was not just a change from plural to singular. Their one God was beyond imagining—no name, no image could contain the one Lord God (see Deuteronomy 6:4). And yet, throughout Scripture, they kept going back to their superhero images. Perhaps the inability to see the negative space for itself is human nature.

We do the same in our present age. We may say we believe in the one Lord God, but, when we pray, do we imagine instead Michelangelo's gray-haired male God—an expropriation of Zeus? Do we see the Lord as true mystery, as negative space, or do we instead misuse our theology to parse and dissect God into a superhero image of our own making?

Jesus' words and actions are filled with images of God and himself, but they are enigmatic and contradictory. Jesus is the Alpha and the Omega, the first and the last; the shepherd and the lamb the master and the slave; the king and the servant; the feeder and the food; the victor and the victim; the judge and the judged; the water and the fire; the priest and the sacrifice; the savior and the scapegoat; death and life. He seems to be saying to us, "Whatever you think that I am, I am that, and I am the opposite as well. I am much more than you can ever imagine. Let go of your graven images of me."

Do we see the Lord as true mystery?

There are many interesting optical illusions based on negative space. For example, the trademark for FedEx® uses the negative space between the "E" and the "x" to create an arrow. If we look at the letters, we cannot see the arrow, but when we concentrate on the negative space and see the arrow, then we no longer see the letters. Perhaps that is what happens when we look at science and faith.

※

As our scientific understanding of the universe has evolved, has our understanding of God evolved to keep pace? Does our negative space (theology) fit with our positive space (science)? The Hebrews adopted the Babylonian understanding of the universe that is described in Genesis. Their universe was a flat supercontinent, floating on a sea of chaos. Over all of this arched the dome of the firmament. Above the dome was heaven, where God resided. The size of their universe was limited to the area they knew (what we now call the Middle East).

The intellectual Greeks had a greatly expanded understanding of the universe. Three centuries before Christ, Aristotle surmised that the Earth was a sphere within a universe of concentric spheres, the lowest being fiery Tartarus and the highest being occupied by the stars. Four centuries later, Ptolemy correctly computed the size of the earth to within a few percentage points and estimated the stars to be 25 million kilometers from the Earth. For the Greco-Romans, that was an almost unimaginable distance, but we now know that the closest planet, Venus, is much farther from us than that.

Perhaps because of this expanded understanding, the Greco-Romans became dissatisfied with their pantheon of superheroes. These anthropomorphic beings were just too small to explain such a vast universe. The unknowable Judeo-Christian God fit better with this new understanding, which may explain their attraction and eventual conversion to the Christian faith. Indeed, faith evolved with science.

Ten centuries after Ptolemy, Dante wrote his *Divine Comedy*, describing an imagined journey through Aristotle's concentric universe. At the center, he replaced the pagan Tartarus with Christian Hell, and at the outermost limits he placed Christian Heaven as the highest sphere, beyond the stars. For the people of his day, Heaven was still a real, physical place in three-dimensional space and time. To deny God a physical location was to deny God's existence.

Two centuries later, when Copernicus published his *Revolution of the Heavenly Spheres*, it went almost unnoticed by theologians, who saw it as just another boring treatise on astronomy. One consequence of his heliocentric theory is that, for it to be consistent with astronomical observations, the stars would need to be immeasurably farther from the earth than Ptolemy had calculated. The known universe therefore became much larger.

The Protestant Reformation emerged around that same time, and with it came theological debates and the need (on both sides) to explain everything. After his death, both Catholic and Protestant leaders condemned Copernicus and his theory. Thus began the tension between faith and science that persists to the present day. Perhaps there is a fear among believers (and a hope among nonbelievers) that science will eventually explain everything, so that nothing will be left to faith.

This fear assumes that the expansion of the positive space of science will displace the negative space of faith. What has happened instead is that, as our knowledge of science has evolved, so has our concept of the divine. The negative space has expanded to match the positive space. The present belief about Heaven, for example, bears little resemblance to the physical location Dante envisaged. Few Christians still believe that God resides in a specific location within three-dimensional space. Instead, we speak of heaven more ethereally, as did Pope John Paul II, who called it "neither an abstraction nor a physical place in the clouds, but a living, personal relationship with the Holy Trinity."[1] We are returning to the original belief in the unknowable one Lord God.

Since the time of Copernicus, our scientific understanding of the universe has grown immensely. Based on Einstein's theory of general relativity, we now know that time, space, and matter are not separate, but are simply different projections of the same reality. A God who creates space and time must be outside of space and time. How can we possibly imagine such a God? The psalmist speaks of this God always in the present tense: "Before the mountains were born, the earth and the world brought forth, from eternity to eternity you are God" (Psalm 90:2).

Scientists now believe that the past is finite. Not only did the universe begin 13.7 billion years ago, but so did time itself. There is no

There in the darkness, in the negative space, is the beginning of everything.

time before then, not even a time with empty space. Cosmologists call this the singularity—a trivial name for something so very profound, but it is better than the popular term, "big bang." Let us instead call it the moment of creation, when everything—all matter, all space, and all time—was in perfect unity in one place at one time. But with time comes change, so before the first trillionth of a trillionth of a second passed, quantum fluctuations caused that perfect unity to begin to divide.

According to quantum mechanics, when one particle divides, the two parts remain entangled, meaning they remain correlated even when separated in space and time. What is truly paradoxical is that the past reality of the particles does not become realized until one of the particles reacts with something else, which is contrary to our notion that the past is entirely determined in the present. When one particle does react with something else, the other one seems to instantly "know" what has happened to its partner. But how can an elementary particle, which has no brain, know anything? Is this mutual knowing with the One Lord God? Does God know all her "children," every single particle in the universe, for all time and all space?

At the moment of creation, everything was perfectly engaged (entangled) with everything else and, since that time, all the particles in the universe have been entangling and re-entangling continuously for 13.7 billion years. That chain of engagement connects everything with everything else endlessly over all space and time. That chain includes us—our bodies, our brains, our friends and our enemies.

In the face of this amazing theory of the cosmos, two questions immediately arise: "How can any God be big enough to create and sustain such a universe?" and "With such an incredible universe, how could there not be a God to create it?" Unfortunately, the theology taught from our pulpits has not caught up with this new science. Our minds cannot see both the positive and negative spaces at the same time—but if we fail to look at the shape of one, we will never see the shape of the other.

※

"THEN GOD SAID, 'Let the water under the sky be gathered into a single basin, so that the dry land may appear.' And so it happened" (Genesis 1:9). Scientists now know that the crust of the earth is made up of tectonic plates. With incredible power, energy from the center of the earth (where Hell used to be) moves whole continents apart. The Red Sea is formed by a plate boundary where the African and Arabian Plates meet. Just east of the Red Sea, in a place once called Midian, lava sometimes wells up to the surface. Long ago, a shepherd in exile from Egypt saw something he did not understand—what appeared to be a burning bush that was not consumed. Looking into the negative space of his understanding, he realized that he was walking on holy ground. Then the one Lord God told him his life's purpose—to challenge the injustice from which he had fled so many years before.

"Then God said, 'Let there be lights in the expanse of the heavens'" (Genesis 1:14). When people look at the night sky, they often marvel at how many stars there are. But when I look up, I see the negative space between the stars. That is where scientists look to detect the cosmic microwave background, the invisible radiance that is as old as the universe itself, traveling continually, without engagement, until it finally engages with the scientists' telescope. In that light, they can see the faint imprint of the quantum fluctuations that occurred at the moment of creation. There in the darkness, in the negative space, is the beginning of everything. And beyond that—beyond space, beyond time—is the one Lord God.

And I must take off my shoes, for I am walking on holy ground. •

Evolving Wild:
Glimpses of the Garden City

By Brittian Bullock and Mike Morrell

A SYMPHONY OF BEGINNINGS

Jesus was under interrogation. In Matthew's Gospel, he was being questioned by teachers of the Law who were attempting to stir up a debate over the merits of marriage and divorce. They advanced an airtight argument for maintaining the status quo by focusing on Moses as the founder of Hebrew culture, and therefore not someone to be questioned.

The framework out of which they were operating might look something like this:

> "We've been doing life this way for a very long time and it's been working fine; how *dare* you question all the progress we've made and the good that's come of it?"

But Jesus refocuses the conversation:

"Moses allowed divorce only as a concession to your hardened hearts—but from the beginning it was not so" (Matthew 19:8, NLT).

"From the beginning" is a curious turn of phrase, is it not? There is a kind of knowing on display here that is impenetrably mysterious. Jesus seems to be suggesting that the human heart has died somewhere along the way. He is also remembering a time when lawful concessions—civilized conventions—did not exist.

A time when the human heart was vibrantly alive.

"From the beginning...."

But which particular beginning? And what of the beginning from which *this* one began?

Ancient Jewish rabbis understood the beginning as an *ex nihilo* event: something from nothing; form out of formlessness. Later, Christian theologians applied the doctrine of grace in much the same way: a gift without reason, no longer tethered to the mimetic system of tit-for-tat or an-eye-for-an-eye.

Such seemingly out-of-nowhere interludes seem plausible within their own coded and storied systems, yet often seem confounding when held up against our lived experience. There is rarely an effect without its cause.

Beginnings seem to be everywhere, if we could but see them clearly enough: a swirl of stardust, the distillation of elements and compounds, world-ending collisions, fiery comets hurtling through far-strung galaxies, countless species and genomes being recycled into the biography and personalities of this present moment.

If it can be said we are created out of nothing, then we are equally created from everything.

Every beginning is a becoming—a transition from one state to another. As Seneca and Semisonic agree: "Every new beginning comes from some other beginning's end."

If it can be said we are created out of nothing, then we are equally created from everything.

HAUNTED HISTORY

WHERE DOES MODERN reflection place our beginnings? Until recently, history books began around ten thousand years ago and focused on Mesopotamia, Egypt, and China, with "Pre-Civilization" taking up perhaps a footnote, or an opening paragraph, at most.

This is the ultimate tail-wagging-the-dog—a thimble-full of water displacing the ocean!

In the past quarter-century, however, a shift has begun—mostly behind the scenes, among dedicated specialists. The fields of linguistics, anthropology, and archeology are reassessing previously sacrosanct value judgments, offering a remarkably different vision of life as it was for the majority of our species' existence.

Recent scholarship has advanced a viable reconstruction of what human life was like "in the beginning," *prior* to the dawn of civilization. It is now argued, with increasing frequency, that our earliest hunter-gatherer ancestors were not the low-browed simians of which memory we hoped to escape, but instead represent an almost-universal state of communal, ecological, and spiritual interdependence.

This resonates with the Genesis narrative, where Adam and Eve embody a symbiotic expression of living in which God and creature are united, lacking self-consciousness (see Genesis 2). In contrast to a Hobbesian vision of early humanity having "no arts; no letters; no society…solitary, poor, nasty, brutish and short,"[1] we witness the original "affluent society."

But if we are "Bible believers," isn't this exactly what we'd expect? The biblical account is of a primal world that is actually "good… good…very good." (Genesis 1). This understanding is mirrored by modern anthropologists who state that Pleistocene-era humans were not separate from the environment, but rather intricately involved in its function. They worked less, played longer, were more interdependent, and lived longer than their early civilized counterparts.

We lived in this interdependent state for one to two hundred thousand years—depending on where we mark the emergence of our species. We've been "civilized"—characterized by a reliance on sedentary living; a cultivated, grain-based diet; and written language—for only the past six to eight thousand years.

If a day is as a thousand years, humanity's collective time in Eden extends far beyond what has happened since then.

PARADIGMS LOST

So where *do* our tradition's sacred texts begin? Lost in the clamor of debates between New Atheism and Old-Time Religion is an elusive, ancient way of reckoning—one that holds the potential to transform our very locus of Scripture's enduring value. In the tussle over historicity or modern scientific accuracy, we've neglected a deeper magic: mythic remembrance that speaks perennially to concerns of the survival and flourishing of our human species, as contained within our gorgeous, turbulent ecosystem. Vital truths have been lost, echoing through a deep well of forgetfulness—insights of life-or-death interest to believer and nonbeliever alike.

But talk of ancient memories is dangerous to the post-Enlightenment positivism of Western culture. For calling our attentions to the past, one is likely to be thought of as advocating ineffective nostalgia at best, or counterproductive, sectarian primitivism at worst. The narrative that our civilization tells is relentless in its pursuit of next steps; it abhors backwardism.

Such critique is valid. There *is* no return to an imagined, pristine state of existence. Such a state can never be re-created; to begin with, it never existed beyond its evocative power. Life is far more complicated than utopian visions of back-in-my-day or once-upon-a-time. Indeed, there is a cherub with a fiery sword guarding Eden against all who seek to go back.

Yet the danger of subscribing to a unidirectional idea of wholesale advancement is that it places us as the victim of forces which have yet to be fully proven. We often forget that evolution contains dead ends and that even forward momentum can stall. As Brian McLaren has observed, the best year to buy a horse and buggy was the one in which the automobile was first invented. Buggy builders had no idea what was coming or how far their stock would eventually drop!

In our rush to progress, we may identify an attractive trend as The Next Big Thing, only to discover—after a decade, century, or millennium—that it is actually an inertia-bound force that keeps us very small indeed.

A dialectical position is required to avoid the pitfalls of primitivism on the one hand and progress-worship on the other. Do we dare drink deeply of our past to fully digest our present, in service of metabolizing a genuinely catalytic evolutionary future?

This is precisely the task before us, sourced in ever-deepening unitive vision and contemplative discernment. The challenge for us, as would-be mystics and change-makers, is to become deep *seers* too, discovering and championing resilient evolutionary growth that honors the Omega Point by taking a fresh—and surprising—look at humanity's Alpha Point.

Big Bangs, Cambrian explosions, and Gospel revolutions have brought us to this stage of our development; what if our Alpha Point is hiding in plain sight?

MYTHIC REMEMBRANCE

A BIBLICAL SCHOLAR of beginnings and endings, Max King, describes biblical prophecy as "symbolic language unveiling the spiritual significance of temporal events."[2] Applying this principle to the Judeo-Christian canon on the whole can be powerfully read as a mythic remembrance of our Spirit-enticed evolutionary becoming, told in poetry, prose, and parable.

This way of remembering brings us face-to-face with the mystery that Jesus reveals in his conflict with the civilized authorities: What killed the human heart, and how do we bring it back to life?

The Hebrew Testament testifies—in both parabolically and anthropologically resonant terms—to the rise of civilization in the Fertile Crescent during the late Neolithic era. It offers vignettes illustrating the end of the abundant world as they knew it alongside the arising of a new world of sowing and reaping, planting and protecting, shoring-up and ruling-over; a lifeway defined by the sweat of the brow.

This trade-off from foraging to farming, from gardening and gathering to hoarding and hiding behind walls, was—in their ancestral memory—a kind of dying.

The New Testament narrative broods over the turbulent face of these social and spiritual tides, offering hidden springs distinct from the totalizing aqueducts of civilization itself: an opportunity to water the seedling signs of a resurgent reality—a Garden City of God.

AT THE SCENE OF A CRIME

What artists, poets, prophets, and mystics existentially grasp, anthropologists, biologists, and geologists are beginning to validate through their sciences: As a species, we've suffered the equivalent of blunt-force trauma—or several episodes in succession; an ancestral, repetitive-stress injury. Indigenous cultures the world over bear witness to this trauma, and it's written between the lines of our own most sacred narratives, often given names like The Fall that conceal as much as they reveal.

What caused this split down the middle of ourselves? What splintered our attentions from the unitive awareness typified in the Tree of Life to the self-reflexive self-consciousness that's the natural-borne fruit of the Knowledge of Good and Evil's tree? What had us abandon over a hundred thousand years' worth of living in symmetry with ourselves and our surroundings, like any other creature of the land, to strike out on our own like the lonely and magnificent, driven and daring, obsessed and exquisite species we experience ourselves to be today?

Was it the decade-long Toba Supervolcano eruption of seventy-five thousand years ago, plunging our planet into a millennia-long cooling period and reducing the human population to a hard-surviving rubble? What of the sweeping extinctions known as the Quaternary period of the Younger Dryas, thirteen thousand years ago? It is widely documented that close to seventy-five percent of the large mammals in North America alone were decimated. Equally large populations were destroyed in Australia, Europe, Asia, and South America during that same epoch. Or, could it be the development of written language or complex agriculture, six to eight thousand years ago?

Now is a time to *wake up* and *grow up* as a species.

The growing consensus is that these are *all* fitting candidates for planetary trauma, and the resultant adaptive technologies that have influenced and altered our developmental trajectory are still being felt. As our species left behind the safety of collective infancy and began navigating the stormy waters of epochal adolescence, our species developed powerful coping techniques to weather these challenges. Civilization itself is a structural container for many of these primary responses, and the fruit—if we're honest—is mixed. Out of a need for increased certainty and security, we integrated agriculture, hierarchy, sexism, militarism, and consumerism. We *also* gave birth to arts, culture, music, and rapid-expansion technologies. The wheat and the tares indeed grow together.

FOUR-FOLD ALIENATION

EVEN AS EXPLORERS of our ancient past are continuing meaningful research into the precise *when* of our collective trauma, our healers, ministers, counselors, and spiritual seers are increasingly clear on the *fact* of our trauma. They're seeing that our reasonable—though maladaptive—responses to it have led to a four-fold fracturing in:

- Our sense of the sacred (God)
- Our own bodies (self)
- Our sense of belonging to the human community (others)
- Our harmony with our environment (world)

If post-civilized humanity's greatest need was a personal ad, it might read like this:

A four-fold alienation from God, self, other, and world is seeking a four-fold reunion with the same. Inquire within.

Taken as a mythic remembrance of our evolutionary becoming, sacred Scripture can be read—powerfully—as chronicling the unraveling effects of civilization upon humanity's relationship with divinity, humanity, community, and ecology. Under these Principalities and Powers, material organization and ingrained consciousness have brought about a catechism of isolation, a habit of separation, and an abiding fear of death.

What can be done to return to wholeness?

The Biblical text describes in vivid detail both the catastrophe and the cure, inviting us to step forward by remembering what was, and is, and is to come. There's a plot-twist, though: Being a product of the very civilization from which it seeks to liberate us, Scripture (along with the Judeo-Christian tradition that houses it, and arguably even the Perennial Philosophy) contains the poison right alongside the cure. This is because the effects of civilization's trauma are ubiquitous; none of the Axial Age religious lineages—East or West—have entirely escaped its dehumanizing, denaturing, and desacralizing influences. In our brilliance and our banality, we're all in this together.

It isn't so much that these turbulent turns have been carte blanche *mistakes*; indeed, as Fr. Richard Rohr so aptly puts it, "everything belongs." Adolescence is, for many, both stormy and catalytic, particularly for those who are described as emotionally sensitive. We first begin to experience genuine talent, creativity, and romantic love, but we feel *everything* cranked up to eleven. Alongside these gifts, we can feel full of rage, depression, and downright destructive impulses—toward our stuff and even ourselves. This is, sadly, an apt description of our planetary mood under civilization. Even so, it isn't so much that we're *wrong* as it is that we're *immature*—making long-term decisions on short-term impulses.

Grace for growth is good parenting, but good parenting also sets boundaries, inspires maturity, and helps develop necessary skills. While a volatile adolescent's swath of destruction is tragic, but limited in scope, a *planet* of developmental adolescents can decimate an entire planet and ecosystem—and we don't have many of those. As Ken Wilber challenges us, now is a time to *wake up* and *grow up* as a species—but how?

The habits, liturgies, and catechisms of *life*—rooted in our ancestral wisdom while reaching into our evolutionary becoming—

are the interventions we need. This is what all healthy religion—its Latin root, *religare*, meaning to bind together—is seeking to do.

Recognizing the depth of our difficulty is the first necessary step in a sober acknowledgment of who we are and why life seems so difficult. Radical acceptance involves seeing where we've come from and just how catastrophic its impact has been in many ways. Even so, we are followers of One for Whom death is not the final word, but, rather, resurrection. Why wouldn't this instinct toward *life* be encoded into our most resonant stories? As a species, we've come precariously close to utter physical extinction at several points in our past. We've experienced multiple bottlenecks where the human population was decimated from millions to a few thousand survivors.

But humanity is still very much alive and breathing.

PERMACULTURE PROMISE

GROWING UP, WE have moved from the infancy of our hunter-gatherer past to the adolescence of our agrarian and civilizational present. Where are we going?

By practicing greater inclusion in our deep-time histories and ecologies, we can let even more light into the aperture of our present awareness. This will help us co-create "the more beautiful world our hearts know is possible," as Charles Eisenstein so evocatively puts it.[3] But we can only discern the poison from the nourishment if we stop swallowing fast-food progress-parables whole. Whether offered by military, government, entertainment, or technology, we're served by first lovingly connecting—to our Source, ourselves, each other, and nature—before sampling the delicacies that we know from experience give us collective heartburn.

Because another world is already here, and it longs to be called forth.

What's curious about this Garden at the beginning of Hebrew Scripture is that it overflows its original banks and boundaries, spilling onto the pages of the rest of the canon. Indeed, there is a shocking similarity between the first two chapters of Genesis and the final two in the Revelation to John. The end and the beginning look remarkably similar—yet with crucial differences. The garden in Genesis becomes a cultivated Garden City in Revelation. The River which flowed through Eden remains, but the elements of gold, pearl, silver, and precious stones have been cultivated, processed, and refined to become the building blocks of the New Jerusalem. The Tree of Life, delicately flowering before Adam and Eve, is now pictured as a massive Vine stretching across its habitat. We are also present there, though we are a transformed species. The vestiges of civilization's stasis prison have been cast off. We need no light, or lamp, or sun-signatures of our obsession with time and efficiency. There is no longer the concession of laws and order, for God has written Divine words upon now-enlivened hearts.

If the human heart was hardened along with the rise of civilization, New Testament authors invite readers to imagine a future that is alive and pulsing with evolutionary remembrance. Jesus' mysterious statement concerning what was "from the beginning" is actually a wake-up call away from our collective amnesia. Many of his hard-to-stomach statements, like "Take no thought as to what you will say" (Luke 12:11), "Consider not what you will eat and drink" (Matthew 6:31), and "Don't store up treasures for yourselves on earth" (Matthew 6:19) find remarkable cohesion with hunter-gatherer living.

This is no lament, but instead an evocation of what was, and is, and is yet to come. Jesus embodies the Garden City—what he calls The Kingdom of God, and what Paul ponders as "life in the Spirit": being fully and deeply here and now in relationship to self, others, Divinity, and all creation.

Digging Deeper: Further Reading

Abram, David. *The Spell of the Sensuous: Perception and Language in a More-Than-Human World*. New York: Vintage, 1996.

Armstrong, Karen. *Fields of Blood: Religion and the History of Violence*. New York: Anchor, 2015.

Berman, Morris. *Wandering God*. New York: State University of New York Press, 2000.

Butler-Bass, Diana. *Grounded: Finding God in the World*. San Francisco: Harper One, 2015.

Cannato, Judy. *Field of Compassion: How the New Cosmology Is Transforming Spiritual Life*. Notre Dame: Sorin, 2010.

Diamond, Jared. *Guns, Germs and Steel: The Fates of Human Societies*. New York: WW Norton, 1999.

Eisler, Riane. *The Chalice and the Blade*. San Francisco: Harper, 1987.

Eisenstein, Charles. *The Ascent of Humanity: Civilization and the Human Sense of Self*. Berkeley: North Atlantic /Evolver Editions, 2013.

---. *The More Beautiful World Our Hearts Know Is Possible* (Sacred Activism). Berkeley: North Atlantic /Evolver Editions, 2013.

Hobbes, Thomas. *The Leviathan*. New York: Penguin, 1982.

King, Max. *The Problem of Time*. Warren, Ohio: Bimillennial Press, 1987.

---. *The Spirit of Prophecy*. Colorado Springs: Bimillennial Press, 2016.

Koch, Paul L; Barnosky, Anthony D. "Late Quaternary Extinctions: State of the Debate." *Annual Review of Ecology, Evolution and Systematics*, 2006: 215-250.

McLaren, Brian. *The Story We Find Ourselves In: Further Adventures of a New Kind of Christian*. San Francisco: Jossey-Bass, 2003.

---. *Everything Must Change: Jesus, Global Crises, & a Revolution of Hope*. Nashville: Thomas Nelson, 2006.

Myers, Ched. "The Fall of Adam and the Rise of Civilization: Brief Notes on Genesis 1–11." Excerpt from "Land Sunday," *The Season of Creation: A Preaching Commentary*. Edited by N. Habel, D. Rhoads, H. Santmire. Minneapolis: Fortress Press, 2011.

---. *The Fall and Anarcho-Primitivism and the Bible*. Entries in *The Encyclopedia of Religion and Nature*. Edited by Bron Taylor. New York: Continuum, 2008.

O'Murchu, Diarmuid. *Ancestral Grace: Meeting God in Our Human Story*. Maryknoll: Orbis, 2008.

---. *In the Beginning Was the Spirit: Science, Religion and Indigenous Spirituality*. Maryknoll: Orbis, 2012.

Plotkin, Bill. *Nature and the Human Soul: Cultivating Wholeness and Community in a Fragmented World*. San Francisco: New World Library, 2007.

Quinn, Daniel. *Ishmael Trilogy: Ishmael, The Story of B, My Ishmael*. New York: Bantam, 1991–1998.

Shepherd, Paul. *Coming Home to the Pleistocene*. San Francisco: Island Press, 2013.

Snodgrass, J. *Genesis and the Rise of Civilization*. Asheville: TJSV Press, 2011.

Wright, Ronald. *A Short History of Progress*. New York: Carroll & Graf, 2005.

Wynward, Todd. *Rewilding the Way: Break Free to Follow an Untamed God*. Harrisonburg: Herald Press, 2015. •

Evidential Medicine for Our Collective Soul

By *Michael Dowd*

RELIGIONS ARE EVOLVING. Nowhere is this more evident than in how spiritual leaders across the spectrum are expanding their views of revelation to include all forms of evidence. We are witnessing the birth of what I have been calling the Evidential Reformation,[1] a time when all forms of evidence (scientific, historic, cross-cultural, experiential) are valued religiously. Crucially, *ecology*—the interdisciplinary study of God's nature—becomes integral to *theology*.

Pope Francis, Patriarch Bartholomew, the Dalai Lama, and the signers of the Islamic Declaration on Global Climate Change are among those spearheading this evidence-honoring *greening of religion*. The movement has been passionate and inspired for decades, but the noble sentiments that spawned *care* for Creation are no match for the crises now spinning out of control.

It is time for a prophetic turbocharging of our religious traditions. Foremost is the need to expand beyond the self-focus of individual salvation or enlightenment to also include vital community concerns—notably, survival. The community now, of course, is the entire human family *and* the more-than-human Earth community.[2]

A renewed call to action cannot be expected to offer pat solutions. Sadly, what were *problems* in the recent past have now exploded into *predicaments*. A predicament (by definition) is a problem for which there are no solutions. It can be neither solved nor overcome, yet it is too impactful to ignore. A predicament must be dealt with conscientiously and continuously. Our responses can offer only more- or less-helpful interventions. The predicament itself will persist.[3]

Once a problem metastasizes into a predicament, forecasts of challenges that *may* arise solidify into disquieting lists of inevitabilities. Such an evidentially derived list is what I offer, in annotated format, in the first part of this essay: "What's Inevitable?"

The second part, "What's Redemptive?" posits that the only way humanity can be "redeemed" is to shift from human-centered to life-centered measures of progress and success. Mythically speaking, this would be *God's prime directive*—expanded into a list of ten Reality's Rules. Underlying these stark (and still very tentative) declarations is a broadening of how we understand "the word of God" today.

WHAT'S INEVITABLE?

I BEGIN WITH A question: *What has God/Reality revealed through evidence about what we can expect in the decades and centuries ahead?* The outlook is surprisingly (and disturbingly) clear. We can expect:

CLIMATE CHAOS[4] — Evidence from a wide range of scientific disciplines now points to escalating climate chaos (global *weirding*) as inevitable. Even if every nation goes *beyond* its 2015 United Nations Framework Convention on Climate Change "COP21" commitments, there is still trouble ahead, notably in the form of intensified storms, droughts, and wildfires; shifts in agricultural zones and habitability; and the breakdown of "environmental services" crucial for maintaining human well-being and civility.

SEA-LEVEL RISE[5] — The last time that the concentration of atmospheric carbon dioxide (CO_2) was 400 parts per million (ppm), the sea level was fifty feet higher than it is today. This was just prior to the Pleistocene glaciations (during which CO_2 hovered around 200ppm). With the sea level having risen mere inches in our lifetimes, though CO_2 is now 405ppm, simplistic logic might tempt us to ignore the past when anticipating our future. This is where the sciences of thermodynamics and glaciology become essential, as they teach us to expect a substantial lag time between cause and consequence. John Englander, former CEO of the Jacques Cousteau Society, sums up our predicament: "What the latest models show is that sea level will continue to rise for at least 500 years, even if we stopped CO_2 emissions immediately."[6] The inevitable loss of our coastal cities was even depicted in the opening ceremony of the 2016 Rio Olympics.[7]

END OF THE FOSSIL-FUEL ERA[8] — Geologists and ecological economists are tracking the depletion of world oil reserves. Exploration and technological advances do not make up for the losses, while the capital and energy costs of finding and producing an additional barrel of oil now exceed what economies can afford to pay. Soon it will be "game over" for high-cost extraction of tar sands, shale fracking, and risky investment in deep-water and polar locales. The end of the fossil-fuel era is thus inevitable, even without governmental intervention to address climate chaos and sea-level rise. Whether "peak oil" has already occurred or is still a few years out is irrelevant. The era of abundant, concentrated energy is behind us; the evidence is compelling. Transitioning to renewables will be expensive, and wrenching[9]—and incapable of powering industries and commerce at today's levels.

Sacrificing for the common good and standing for the future must be honored as sacred.

Political Unrest[10] — Climate chaos, sea-level rise, and the decline of cheap, concentrated, easily transportable energy will interact to undermine the well-being of ordinary citizens. Even nations with strong economies, high ground, vast agricultural acreage, and social cohesion will be vulnerable. Political unrest and turmoil will be unavoidable. The evidence of history points toward severe disruptions that will force economies, governance, and cultures to re-localize—that is, to contract in scope and scale. There will be suffering and loss—but also opportunities for finding meaningful work and forging cooperative relationships in real communities. Economic contraction will unburden youth who have been victims of what environmental sociologist William Catton calls the Age of Exuberance. Once again, *real* work will be available for young adults. Apprenticeships will increasingly replace classroom modes of education. Earlier entry into adult activities that build self-esteem will diminish the lure of addictive substances and errant activities that now challenge youth who, necessarily, choose to isolate or socialize mostly with same-age peers.

Toxic Legacy[11] — Historians and ecologists have documented the harmful impacts that virtually all civilizations have had on the health and recycling services of the ecosystems on which they depend. The reverberating effects on public health, economies, and safety become disastrous. In the inimitable words of Robert Louis Stevenson, "Sooner or later we all sit down to a banquet of consequences."[12] Additional burdens bequeathed to our descendants include nuclear waste, heavy metals, and toxic chemicals that will endure in the biosphere for centuries, even millennia. Climate-driven sea-level rise will exacerbate the problem. The landward ingress of corrosive saltwater will penetrate metal containments. Ground flows and ocean currents will then disperse the poisonous contents. Equally, a superabundance of CO_2 becomes a toxin in its own right by acidifying seawater, threatening species whose shells depend on ocean alkalinity. Biologists report that severe marine degradation is already underway.

Biodiversity Catastrophe[13] — Since the late 1970s, when biologists warned that human impacts had triggered the Sixth Mass Extinction, species recovery and habitat improvements have been overwhelmed by escalating losses at the global level. Now conservation biologists are facing a future in which even common species (especially plants) will require our help in moving poleward at a pace that far exceeds their own capacities. That looming need for "assisted migration"[14] will, however, coincide with reluctance in stressed societies for channeling funds toward any activities beyond immediate human needs. Thus, threatened species in even the wealthiest nations face an uphill battle.

CULTURAL LOSS[15] — In times of stress, the complexities that weave communities into civilizations falter. When individuals and societies struggle to secure basic needs, the arts and sciences that both create *and* depend on high culture suffer. In such times, there will be those who voluntarily sacrifice their own comfort and security in service of safeguarding cultural treasures through a dark age. "Love something, learn something, let something go, and pass something forward" is how I regularly encourage audiences to embark on a legacy project.

WORLDVIEWS UNRAVELING[16] — If any of the above inevitabilities were news to you, you likely experienced a twinge of one or more of *the five stages of grief*. These are denial, anger, bargaining, depression, and acceptance—acceptance leading not merely to acquiescence, but also to what Joanna Macy calls "active hope." When worldviews unravel there is loss, and the grieving process is instinctive and healthy. A traditional and vital function for religions in the future will thus be to shepherd individuals through the emotional and faith challenges that accompany periods of societal stress, when expectations erode and meanings unravel. As more and more people discover that their expectation of never-ending progress is an illusion, and as disruptions spread, religions will be called upon to do what they've always done: help people live meaningful lives, foster healthy relationships, die peacefully, and leave a sweet legacy.

To stay relevant for the times, religions will need to foster not only *personal wholeness* and *social coherence*. The exemplary wisdom of indigenous peoples is also crucial. *Ecological integrity*—right relationship to primary reality: God's nature, the literal ground of our being—must be central.[17] Sacrificing for the common good and standing for the future must be honored as sacred.

WHAT'S REDEMPTIVE?

REDEMPTION FOR HUMANITY does not imply that we can undo or compensate for the ecological devastation we have already wrought. We can, however, set out on a new course. We, the prodigal species, can come home to reality, come home to God.

Whether framed in secular or religious language, the implications are clear. If we treat primary reality as anything other than primary, there will be consequences—if not immediately, then compounded in the future. Voiced religiously, the health and well-being of God's nature comes first. Anything else is human-centered, and thus a form of idolatry.

Anthropocentrism and the myth of human omnipotence over primary reality have brought forth a global economic system that rewards the few at the expense of the many, measures progress by how fast it can pollute the biosphere, and forces billions to betray posterity in pursuit of the so-called "good life." Whether we call such an anti-future economy unsustainable, insane, or demonic, really doesn't matter; it has no future. What is not aligned with God's nature is self-terminating. There can be no human progress so long as Earth's soils, waters, air, and life are degraded.

Ecologically, the success of any species begins with learning to thrive within the limits of *carrying capacity*. Humanity's drawdown of natural resources and polluting of natural systems are not exempt from this law of life. How many fish can be harvested without depriving our descendants of sustenance in the future? How much petroleum can be burned without triggering runaway climate catastrophe?

It is time to integrate carrying capacity into our theologies. Toward this end, I now speak of "grace limits." The bounds that delimit safe levels of human use of other creatures and their habitats are defined by natural grace. By staying within those bounds, we experience the grace of God's nature. When we venture beyond—which we have done, excessively—we suffer "God's wrath" via storms, drought, floods, wildfires, rising and acidifying oceans, and in another Great Dying of species.

The call to action for religious adherents is this: to first learn about, then reflect upon, and finally evolve our worldviews. Henceforth, *the unbending grace limits of God's nature*, combined with carrying

Ecologically, the success of any species begins with learning to thrive within the limits of *carrying capacity*.

capacity deficits inflicted by a century of human overpopulation and extravagant consumption,[18] will constrain even our noblest aims and thus the bounds of our efforts.[19]

Idealism will be tempered whenever human *problems* morph into the far more dangerous and intractable contours of *predicaments*. The onset of multiple crises, such as those we witness today, signals that we have arrived at just such a turn.

I personally have spent much of the past three years revising and mourning the loss of a techno-optimist worldview that inspired my bright-eyed "evolutionary evangelism" for nearly two decades. Along the way, I've been blessed, not only with active hope, but also with a revised action plan that nourishes my soul. It feeds my soul because it arises from a realistic assessment of my own gifts and limitations at this pivotal time.

Among the tangible outcomes of my new focus is an uncompromising to-do list for humanity, which I offer below. This list derives from the collective intelligence of hundreds of scientific and religious colleagues with whose ideas I have wrestled and who have wrestled with mine.[20]

For a religiously progressive audience, this set of declarative statements may be controversial, not so much for *what* it says, but *how*. Because "the *evidential* word of God" includes the knowledge and wisdom born of science, history, and cross-cultural experience,[21] I have no difficulty writing *as if* the commanding, no-nonsense, biblical God were speaking today. Crucially, in offering these "Ten Commandments," I am *not* channeling an otherworldly entity, nor am I accessing esoteric wisdom. Rather, I am aggregating scholarship in science, history, and cross-cultural studies to give voice to global collective intelligence in a way that maps our way home.

However you may respond to the style and tone of what follows, know that my proposal is a poor cousin to the power and art of what Conservation International and a dozen Hollywood stars have already achieved. Please take a few minutes to watch one or more of the "Nature Is Speaking" videos, freely available online, some of which have gone viral.[22] These short, one- to two-minute videos are unsurpassed for conveying the prophetic power of *personification*—giving human characteristics to what is more-than-human.[23]

REALITY'S RULES

TEN COMMANDMENTS TO AVOID EXTINCTION AND REDEEM HUMANITY

THE ORIGINAL TEN Commandments, as well as this version, delineate *the limitations on our behavior essential for human communities to persist over the long term*. Just as the Hebrew commandments were guidelines for a troubled people in a challenging time, the set below articulates the *constraints* that our species must now impose on itself while navigating crises of our own creation.

The first five commandments strive to inoculate us against the all-too-common virus of idolatry—that is, an unreal notion of God, a divinity not consistent with reality. The second five offer a clear and compelling way back into right relationship to primary reality. Each is intended to be heard in the first person, as God speaking.[24] In traditional religious language,

Thus sayeth the Lord . . .

1. Stop thinking of me as anything less than the voice of undeniable and inescapable reality.
2. Stop thinking of "revelation" or "divine instruction" without including evidence.
3. Stop thinking of Genesis, or your creation story, apart from the history of the universe.
4. Stop thinking of theology apart from ecology: the interdisciplinary study of my nature.

5. Stop defining and measuring "progress" in short-term, human-centered ways.
6. Stop allowing the free or subsidized polluting of the commons.
7. Stop using renewable resources faster than they can be replenished.
8. Stop using non-renewable resources in ways that harm or rob future generations.
9. Stop exploring for coal, oil, and natural gas—keep most of it in the ground.
10. Stop prioritizing the wants of the wealthy over the needs of the poor.

CODA

THE CHALLENGES AHEAD threaten to overwhelm, yet I am moved to tears of joy as often as tears of sorrow. What a time to be alive and awake! What an honor to be engaged in the Great Work[25] of fostering a mutually enhancing human-Earth relationship! Supporting one another through the stages of grief and inevitable challenges along the way is surely medicine for our collective soul. •

Mystic Love, Unbound:

A Reclaimed, Reframed, and Evolving Love Story between God and the World

By Teresa Pasquale Mateus

PART 1: THE EVOLUTION OF SCIENCE

ONE OF THE most precious words to me is neuroplasticity. Simply defined, it means the brain can change.[1] What a beautiful revelation of science—and one that the mystic tradition has been teaching forever. The gift of science—neuroscience, psychobiology, and beyond—is that it is beginning to catch up with these mystical mysteries of the universe.

The science of the sacred, and neuroplasticity specifically, has had profound effects in my own life and healing process (from trauma, loss, and illness) as well as in my role as a trauma therapist. We get hopeless and fearful. We forget what our brain inherently knows: We can change. I explain neuroplasticity to my clients this way: "Your brain has proven it can change once already, because it changed in response to your trauma. All we have to do is the work to help it change again."

It is amazing how empowering it is for someone to understand that science reveals to them their inner truth—that they have the power to change their path. That is the beauty of the evolving revelations of science. We can now point to the mysteries of the universe, expressed in our personhood, as they light up on a screen or are illustrated in data. We can offer people the concrete understanding of ancient wisdom in a palatable form. There is something, in the knowing and being known I see illustrated in this science of our brain and the study of our heartbeats, that makes me, as a therapist and a novice neuroscience nerd, feel more intimately connected to God.

For instance, mirroring neurons, which we can now track with brain scans and heart math, which we can register with heart rate variability (HRV) trackers, illustrate to us the inherent interconnectedness we have with each other and the sentient beings in our midst.[2] The study of brain and heart show that, when we are in deep relationship with one another, we actually synchronize—so much so that the mirroring neurons in our brain and the HRV rhythm of our heart will begin to function in unison with each other—thereby making the distinction between the individual me and the "other" less and less distinguishable as we connect.[3]

The historic mystics understood this interconnectedness of self with the wider world. It translated from their intimate experiences of God outward into richer experiences of others. Now, if we choose to, we can point and see how connected we have the potential to be.

This also reinforces the intentionality of the contemplative path as communal rather than individualistic. It is not a singular experience I

Like a love story, we are moving from our romantic notion of a distant God into the intimacy of true love.

am offered—to keep for myself—but, rather, a gift of deep relationship I am meant to share with others. Unfortunately, much of the contemporary contemplative tradition, perhaps most influenced by our Western individualism, has become diminished down to our personal selves, our personal practices, our personal transformations. What was once as big and interconnected as the whole universe, as interpersonal as Jesus' words in Matthew 25:40 (NIV), "Whatever you did for one of the least of these brothers and sisters of mine, you did for me," has become Westernized. We have limited the intended expansiveness and inclusion, embodiment and action, and have turned the vastness of the mystic experience into a line of picket fences, dividing the space between my personal spirituality and yours.

Evolution is also sometimes about a return, a re-visioning, a re-membering of what was for a new place and time. In many ways, the evolution of our scientific knowing over the history of the human experience has just been the re-membering of a history of the world that always existed. We just hadn't consciously acknowledged its truths. Like a love story, we are moving from our romantic notion of a distant God into the intimacy of true love, which has depth, and whose reality is much greater than the surface-layer understanding. Neuroplasticity, mirroring neurons, and heart math are here to help us re-member our potential for connection, for change, for transformation in love, with one another and with God. We are called to go inward so we can come out into the world and be changed; so that we can change the world itself, together.

PART 2: THE EVOLUTION OF THE CONTEMPLATIVE

IN JAMES 2:17 (NKJV), we are reminded of our call to action, as people of faith, to a world in pain: "Thus also faith by itself, if it does not have works, is dead."

In this time and place, how do we embody and enliven this call? What does contemplation without works look like? What does contemplation with works look like? The world is calling the Christian contemplative lineage to erupt and evolve out of the small container of personal spirituality into active relationship with the world. There is an urgency to it. The world offers us this urgency. The urgency is scary. The call often feels too vast.

How do we love those who have the least, but need the most, in a way that moves beyond prayer, beyond the inner love story between us and God, and illustrates God's love in the world? How do we support those who struggle daily to seek equality in systems of power constructed to subvert all attempts for equality? This evolution of the world in which we live calls for an evolution of the mystic path and the way that we see, seek, and become the beloved community in the world. It calls for us to embody our contemplative path in a new way. It calls for our physical bodies to come in contact with the pain of the world and be activated for change. Our evolving contemplative path is the true intersection of justice, healing, and contemplative spirituality—one that Jesus, as well as many of our mystic predecessors, have walked.

We can reclaim the ancient stories of embodiment, empowerment, and action that come from our own lineage. We often forget the embodied and revolutionary saints and mystics that followed in Jesus' path: St. Francis, stripping before the bishop as an embodied act of solidarity with the poor; Teresa of Ávila, pushing against the establishment of monasticism in her Carmelite order, under threat of punishment and violence from the Spanish Inquisition, to revolutionize her order; John of the Cross, tortured and imprisoned for his participation and championing of Teresa's monastic revolution; Julian of Norwich, dedicating her life to giving counsel and emotional support to all who came to her door, hurting and broken by the suffering and aftermath of the Black Plague. With every deeper calling into intimacy with the Beloved, they were equally, if not more radically, called into communion with the aching world. The evolution of their souls was not a solitary process. The deep love story that called them inward, called them just as powerfully outward again, sacrificing time with the Beloved to serve those whom the Beloved loved.

The reason they worked so hard to engage their contemplative love with action-as-love in the world is because the world is deeply in need of the contemplative wisdom. There are so many Christian people deeply yearning for what the contemplative path has to offer—but often there is a great divide between the prayer circles and the activists, the people of faith in communities of color and the contemplative retreats. The spaces seem remote and inaccessible to many who need them the most: those suffering from poverty and homelessness; those on the frontline of protests and marches for justice; those who sit in non-contemplative church contexts, who were alienated from the contemplative lineage by their distance from the Catholic tradition and culture. Each are deeply yearning for a love affair with God, but do not have the language or the tools to access the source material, nor are they able to relate to the nature of the current contents in the contemplative container. Further, members of each group carry practices from their own traditions and cultures that could serve the current contemplative containers—rituals of healing from street protests, mantras of lament and hope from those in the margins, and prayers and songs from African and indigenous cultures—carrying organic mysticism in their every practice.

The existing practices and models of contemplative Christianity—having been resuscitated from Christianity's lineage in the 1970s by monastic wisdom elders—were never meant to fit the needs of the current context. They were created to meet the needs of a predominantly home-based spiritual practice that was tangible and understandable, but specifically crafted for a white, upper-middle-class contingent. It served well at the time. It created a great tide that has carried contemplative Christianity into the present. It is, however, a container that has become too small.

Most specifically, for people existing in the margins—who desperately need contemplative wisdom—a path of contemplation without action, and often specifically without activism, doesn't have meaning. Because their struggles are for survival, for themselves, their loved ones, and their communities, these struggles cannot be set aside in pursuit of an individual spiritual journey. The journey is inherently communal. It is inherently one of struggle. It necessitates action, but desperately seeks contemplation.[4] The current contemplative container was not built for them and cannot contain their hurts, their actions, their needs, their identities.

Only together can we push through to the next phase of our spiritual evolution.

When the container is too small for the contents, it must expand. It must evolve. Today's Christian contemplative container must evolve—because the contents are the whole of Christianity and the whole of the body of Christ, and currently not everyone can fit.

It is time to build a container wide enough for all the expressions of the contemplative lineage as they are being called forth in this time. This is about reclaiming ancient wisdom. It is about seeing that wisdom through new eyes. It is about the breadth and depth of the fullness of God's love being expressed among all God's people—and for us to see that this divine, mystical story of love, like all love, doesn't just look like *my* love story. It looks like a thousand different love stories, all coming from and returning to the same root—the Divine.

PART 3: THE EVOLUTION OF US, TOGETHER

We *are* the evolution in process. We *are* the biological evolution of our physical selves, becoming more than we have been able to be before. We *are* the scientific evolution in our time, which is beginning to find its symbiosis with the ancient wisdoms of mysticism—the indwelling knowing and unknowing revealing itself to us in the mapping of brains and the scanning of hearts. We *are* the contemplative evolution, becoming what it always was and always was intended to be—the intimate love story with God calling us to be embodied and communal. The call comes from deep inside the pain of the world—the injustice, inequality, denigration, and degradation, the suffering in impoverished nations and on city streets—to act out loud and act now to manifest this sacred love story into all dimensions of humanity.

The neuroplasticity of our brains reminds us we have the capacity to change and evolve, even the structure of our minds and the nature of our thoughts. Each moment is an opportunity for growth. Each moment is a chance to mirror connectedness in our brains and our hearts, not just to God, but also to one another. Science illuminates the great creation of God, built into each of us for a divine purpose—to change, to connect, and to grow in communion with each other.

God's great love story with us calls us into *discomfort*—the gateway to evolution. For the majority culture, this call is to be in the margins, alongside marginalized persons, and learn what is needed to authentically walk beside them in their suffering. It calls for the discomfort of being in spaces where the mystical path may not look like your own—to be witness to the panoply of ways that God has written the contemplative story throughout Christianity. It calls for the discomfort of hearing God's voice through the woman of color, the queer teen, the under-heard and under-seen in many contemplative spaces—and to reorient perspectives and actions according to the lessons taught through deep listening in these new spaces. For people of color, like myself, and others in the margins (women, LGBTQI, and beyond), it is also a time to let our voices rise and join this conversation as vital partners in the unfolding of this new evolution in the collective soul of contemplative faith.

In the process, together, we co-create the contemplative evolution and the mystical revolution, along with *all* our brothers and sisters of faith that God is calling forth in this moment and time. In a world in pain, we are in the crescendo of birthing ourselves for this place and time. Only together can we push through to the next phase of our spiritual evolution.

Fr. Richard Rohr beckons us, in the Introduction to this edition of *Oneing*, into "this newness and moreness of which we are afraid." It is where all the beauty and surprise lie, of God's becoming and our becoming, in this world. It is in the unfolding moreness that we find the evolving expression of God's love for us, and our courage to return that love into and unto the world. •

The Evolution of Love

By Tasha Wahl

None would go freely, if we knew ahead of time what love is going to ask of us.
—Richard Rohr

I HAVE A LOVE STORY to tell. It is not the fairy tale I dreamed as a young girl. It's not the beautiful and shining castle in the sky I built as a young woman. In fact, those stories and dreams had to die and the castle had to tumble down before the true love story could be told: my story.

Relationships are, in a sense, defined by expectations. Growing up as a child in the United States in the 1970s, my expectations were shaped by my family, but also by my culture. Movies, books, television, and the covers of magazines all helped to inform what I wanted in relationships, and especially what I wanted love and marriage to look like. Of every relationship I had, I pinned my highest hopes and dearest dreams on a marriage, the terms of which I'd built up in my mind. The man I married would be my partner for life. We would stand strong, defying every tempest life brought our way. When you looked in the dictionary at the word love, our story would be the ultimate definition. The two of us would change the world with our love.

I think most of us would agree that our expectations are high for marriage. This is fair, as the person we marry is intended to be the one with whom we spend the majority of our sleeping—if not waking—hours. At the altar, we promise to have and to hold, no matter what, 'til death do us part. What we usually don't say at the altar is, "I promise to love you even though the person I am standing with today will evolve and change into a different person many times in the course of this partnership—and I will change just as many times over the years."

WHO ARE WE?

I HAVE BEEN MARRIED for twenty-two years to multiple men—dozens, maybe even hundreds. They are all named Erik, but they are as unique as the stars in the sky. I have learned to love them all.

My husband, likewise, has married many, many versions of me, which reflect every color of the rainbow, and every subtle shift in hue between the colors.

We're like a movie in my mind: twenty-two years of history, twenty-two years of letters, twenty-two years of pictures and videos, twenty-two years of growing a family together.

Life is a series of changes, and yet most of us resist. We want things to be comfortable. We want to travel the path of least resistance.

I have learned over the years to embrace the evolution of Erik, including the men he has yet to become and the ideas and ideals he has yet to embrace.

But in order to get to this place, I had to give up something that I thought I never could. I had to give up love as I knew it, or thought I knew it, and I had to learn to embrace a new kind of love: one without expectations, without a known outcome, a love that released Erik to be who he is and not who I needed him to be.

I have learned to stop trying to hold him to being the man I married.

The biggest surprise in all of this is that the main person standing in the way of this new love was *me*. I was the one who needed to evolve from my old ways of thinking. I had to let go of the expectations, the images, the ideals I had spent my life building. That is a lot of undoing—a lot of "unthinking," as we like to say around our house—and deprogramming.

The evolution of my love took many years and I know I have many more years to grow. But, as so much change is preceded by crisis, I had to come to the end of myself before I was willing to release dreams so they could evolve into something new. I lived many dark nights of the soul, arguing with my own ego about what I could and couldn't do. Eventually my True Self, the God in me, helped me to see that I can do hard things—even when that meant giving up the dreams I thought I had to have.

I had to redefine the change I thought I wanted in Erik. I had to learn that this wasn't about the man I needed him to be. It was about the wife I needed to be. The evolution of this new love was apparently my ability to let go of the love that I thought I had to have. The hardest part of that process was letting go of the identity that I had built up around who that love made me.

WHOSE ARE WE?

THIS NEW WAY of loving also changed my relationship with how I prayed. I had spent my life praying lovingly for a specific outcome, the outcome that I thought was best, as in, "I mean I know how to love well, so please, please, please bring out the best in Erik." But what I came to understand was that I was praying for the best Erik for *me*, for the best *us*.

God will glorify our marriage in His way. Instead of praying for a certain outcome, I now pray that I release the outcome. I focus on me being grateful for the now, for the good moments and the difficulties. We don't grow without the death of our old selves, and our partners have to die to their selves in order to become new too.

I used to tread with fear and trepidation over a change of job, a change of finances, a change in our health. I feared that anything Erik did that was different than my heart dictated would draw us apart. He and I being on different pages would send me into a tailspin.

When he "hurt my feelings," usually unintentionally, just speaking his truth, I was wounded like a bird shot in the chest. When your spouse is your identity, you can't allow him to hurt you. It's like dying.

I have had to learn to see Erik without a filter, without a binary "good" or "bad" judgment. He can't be my "everything" because he isn't perfect. If I hold onto the idea that if I am not loved perfectly I am not worthy, life becomes painful. Erik can be good, and not perfect. He can do things that wound me, and that doesn't make him a bad person.

I've learned that in my marriage, in the middle of a large crisis or even just an argument, my ego takes over. I am protective of my side of the story, my need to be right, my fear of losing. When I can step away and breathe, when I can even just notice myself reacting, I can stop the story in my head long enough to gather perspective—and know that I'm seeing things the way *I am*, not the way *they are*.

Whenever possible, I stop and I try to find the incarnate, the cosmic Christ, in me—my True Self—and I ask that the God in me be glorified in the situation. I ask not that the other person would change, but that *my* perspective would change—that I would be able to speak truth and love, and not speak my opinion or my narrative.

This practice is called many things, but I love the word "mindful." I become mindful of staying in the present moment, of not holding on to the hurts of the past or fear of the future. I just breathe, feeling my body and being mindful of the moment. The other person is another human being with whom I have quantum entanglements. I've learned to ask myself this question at the first sign of trouble: "What is the most loving thing I can do?"

EMBRACING RESTORATIVE LOVE

THE OLDER I become, the more I am learning to embrace an evolutionary love, one that replenishes itself and restores me.

Relationally, we have to understand we are ruled by our emotions. The only way to overcome our emotions is to name them, observe them, and quietly love them. Then we become mindful in the moment.

This takes years of practice, but we're offered dozens of opportunities each day to practice being mindful, to practice restorative love. We can learn to pray that God would show us how we can change, would teach us how our hearts can break for the other, so we begin to see through His eyes.

> I try to find the incarnate, the cosmic Christ, in me—my True Self—and I ask that the God in me be glorified in the situation.

When Erik began to travel around the world for long periods of time, we learned that talking on the phone was nearly impossible, between the time difference and our inability to simultaneously be in a place where we could speak meaningfully. So we began to write letters.

Those letters have become an archive of our evolution as man and woman, as a couple, as parents and business partners. I've saved them all. Those letters tell stories that I can't even remember. They have preserved arguments I didn't even know we had, including business ideas that never saw the light of day, and hopes and dreams and fears. They contain the evolution of our parenting, our faith, and our beliefs.

As I read them, I know that, at the time, I passionately believed in everything I wrote. Every single me I have ever been comes to life in those letters and emails. And they have taught me something: I tend to act and react in the moment. The story I am telling myself when I'm in the moment is all I can see—and I react to that story, be it good or bad, true or false. I react.

I've learned in the last few years to sit quietly and watch myself and my emotions. I remind myself they are just that—emotions. I remind myself that Erik and my boys are also emotional beings, sharing themselves in the world.

So, as I learn to sit in mindfulness and meditation, I can name those emotions and learn to hold the pain that comes with many of them. I am learning that FEAR is an acronym for what's happening in my mind: False Evidence Appearing Real.

Non-dual thinking allows me to have grace, for myself and for Erik. The man I used to think was perfect in every way doesn't need to be perfect anymore.

We can hurt each other with words; sometimes that's an unavoidable reality. He can "sin" and still be good. I can "fail" and still be successful. It's not "either/or," it's "yes, and."

And I can accept that he is going to be a different person in five years than he is today. I don't need to hold on tightly to the past, to who we used to be. I need to understand that to love and cherish and have and hold means to hold lightly—sometimes even to release. When I am most afraid, inevitably, the monsters turn out to be shadows in my head.

THE REST OF THE STORY

This I pray:

- That I might reflect God in my marriage and all other areas of my life: work, parenting, friendship.
- That the God in me would be stronger than me.
- That the restorative love of God would be stronger than the retributive love of my ego.
- That I can be mindful of myself and my shadow self, and accepting of the other's shadow self.

My story now is not about a husband and a wife. It's about God's love for me. It's also about my ability to stop needing others to change, but rather being the change I want to see in the world.

My story continues, as I never give up hope for God's glory and love, which is always restorative and forgiving.

Ultimately, there is freedom in letting go of the dreams and living in the now.

My story, and all the men in it, is a far more interesting story than the one I thought I wanted, because this story is a living, changing evolution of love.

I am looking forward to the next thousand chapters. •

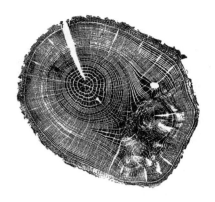

Instinctual Biases:
How Understanding Our Evolutionary Past Can Help Free Us from Our Cage

By Mario Sikora

MY WIFE RECENTLY picked me up at the airport as I returned from yet another trip away. It had been a long day—I hadn't had much sleep during the past week and was up early to get to the airport in time for my flight. I find that even flying for only a few hours is increasingly unpleasant these days.

Tanya and I were happy to see each other and, as we drove home, she told me all that I had missed while I was away: The washing machine had broken and flooded the basement (which I knew because she had called me in the midst of it); the handyman had come to repair the garage door and some electrical fixtures; a shingle or two had blown off the roof during a sudden and severe storm; our second son had an eye exam that indicated he needs glasses; she didn't get a chance to do the grocery shopping. . . .

I made mental notes on each of these things, hoping to remember anything that required intervention or action from me, but the truth is that my mind was elsewhere. I tried not to give that impression, as these matters are important to Tanya—which means they are important to me. But had she not talked about them, I would not have asked. I was more focused on the trip from which I had just returned—the meetings I had attended, the people I had met, the implications of those interactions for my work.

In time, she asked how my trip had gone, and I started talking about the people I had been with and the city I had just left. She listened politely.

When we arrived home, we were greeted by Alexei, the third of our four sons. Alexei asked me about my trip. Though I'd told him my location multiple times while I was away, he had no idea where I had just been. He quickly launched into telling me all about his new sneakers. All of ten years old, Alexei likes sneakers and his goal is to have a different pair for each day of the week. He's an outgoing and talkative boy, and since the time he could walk he has been drawn to vivid clothing and fashion accessories, as well as nice cars and fancy houses. Alexei is a rough-and-tumble boy, like his brothers, but he has always had style.

Some may read these paragraphs and think these are typical exchanges between members of a normal family: A husband and wife who love each other and have learned to show interest in what matters to the other, even when it might require effort; a son who missed his father and was eager to reconnect after a week apart. But such a surface reading would miss something deeper: patterns that affect many relationships—marriages, families, friendships, and business partnerships. What was happening below the surface of each exchange were conversations that occur when we have different "instinctual biases"—patterns of focus and values rooted in our evolutionary heritage.

Our values—what we consider to be important—determine how we live our lives and how we treat others.

Our values—what we consider to be important—determine how we live our lives and how we treat others. Almost all conflicts are rooted in a clash of values: a sense that others have the wrong values or that our values are not being respected. Understanding these instinctual biases and how they influence our behaviors can profoundly change the way we experience ourselves, others, and the world—and how we can improve our relationships and sense of well-being. In this article, I would like to introduce the three instinctual biases and ways to manage them more effectively so we are no longer ruled by them.

The concept of *instinctual biases* has evolved from the Enneagram model of personality styles—a profound system for observing our habitual patterns, which are rooted in nine distinct adaptive strategies. Enneagram theory holds that each of the nine personality "types" or "Ennea-types" can be further divided into three "subtypes," variations based on the disproportionate influence of an instinctual "energy." These "energies" are commonly referred to as "self-preservation," "social," and "one-to-one" or "sexual."

Current theories about the subtypes are rooted in either a neo-Freudian model or the Gurdjieffian tradition. Being science-minded, I am uncomfortable with the vagueness of these frameworks and prefer to think about these patterns of attention as *clusters of evolutionary adaptions*—behaviors or cognitive mechanisms that helped our ancestors survive long enough to reproduce.

To understand the three instinctual biases, it may help to imagine a documentary about peacocks.

- The first segment of the documentary focuses on "self-preservation" or the Preserving Domain—behaviors related to nesting and nurturing. It shows how the peacock builds its nest, gathers food, keeps itself clean and healthy, and nurtures its offspring.

- The second segment focuses on the "social" or Navigating Domain—behaviors related to how the peacock orients itself to the group. It shows how the peacock determines its territory, learns the mores of the flock (or "muster"), and finds its place in the pecking order.

- The third segment of the documentary focuses on the "sexual" (one-to-one) or Transmitting Domain—behaviors related to how the peacock gets the attention of the peahen so they can make peachicks. It shows the loud calling of the peacock and its display of feathers to demonstrate its health and robustness.

Humans are more complicated than peacocks, of course, but in many ways our fundamental instinctual needs are pretty much the same—we need to preserve the resources we need to survive, figure out how to get along with the rest of the tribe, and seem desirable to potential mates. Our evolutionary heritage has done us a service by equipping us with deeply rooted inclinations to do these things.

But we live in a different world than our ancestors, and the adaptations that served *them* so well can sometimes work against *us*.

Our ancestors had to scrounge for food and sustenance, while most of us are fortunate enough to have access to more food than we could ever eat. Biologists call such abundance a "supernormal" stimulus, which overwhelms the response mechanism that has evolved to respond to it. Those of us in the developed world easily fall into consuming more and more resources of all kinds in an attempt to satisfy a false void created by a blind, instinctual need for "enough" that developed at a time in human history when truly getting "enough" was a daily struggle.

Our ancestors needed to study the tribe and its mores to better navigate the social hierarchy. For us, on the other hand, technology has geometrically expanded the size of our "tribe." We have become obsessed with the lives of those at the top of the hierarchy, fixating on the social and romantic lives of celebrities rather than going outdoors and talking to our neighbors. We now more frequently socialize in and navigate through a virtual world rather than a physical one.

Our ancestors figured out ways to enhance their desirability through accomplishment, adornment, or charm and charisma. Our instinctual need to transmit has given rise to a narcissistic "selfie" and "sexting" culture.

Each of these instinctual biases can manifest at cultural and national levels as well—in the form of tribalism, self-centeredness, and a collective fear of insufficient resources that leads to war and ethnic hatred. Allowing our instinctual biases to run roughshod in the shadows creates a spiritual crisis for humanity.

We live in a different world than our ancestors, and the adaptations that served them so well can sometimes work against us.

I DON'T WANT TO paint too bleak a picture here; nothing about human nature is writ in stone and we can rebel against and perhaps even tame our animal nature. But we cannot escape the cage we do not see or understand, so it is helpful to recognize that these instinctual behaviors arose in us as responses to the survival and reproductive needs of our ancestors.

The fact that they are so deeply rooted in our psyche should create in us a feeling of self-compassion. Viewed in this light, our "sins" make sense. We fall victim to our instinctual biases, not because we are weak, but because they are powerful and, in a different environment, necessary. That we can see the origin and context of these impulses makes it possible to overcome their hold on us.

Like most social species, we humans tend to specialize, finding roles and strengths that allow us to make a contribution to the group. Thus, each of us has a bias toward one of these instinctual domains, focusing a disproportionate amount of our attention on the needs it represents. Some of us are biased toward preserving, some toward navigating, and some toward transmitting. While this short article cannot cover this dimension of our nature in depth, what follows is a brief description of each instinctual bias and some suggestions for paying attention as we work with them.

PRESERVING: Those with a dominant bias toward Preserving tend to focus on ensuring that they, and those they care about, have sufficient food, shelter, and the myriad other resources that not only sustain life but also make it comfortable. They are attuned to needs related to their health and well-being and they are often collectors or cultivators of the traditions and artifacts that create a sense of continuity with the past. They can fall into the trap of overdoing their preserving tendencies, never feeling that they have quite enough of what they need, fearing that something may disrupt their comfort and well-being, or believing that resources are scarce even when they are not.

Navigating: Those with a dominant bias toward Navigating tend to focus on the workings of the group and their status in it. They want to understand the group hierarchy, the interrelationships of the members of the group, and how they can better fit into it. They are "soft networkers" who don't push themselves on others, but maintain connection with a broad and loose network that allows for a flow of information about trust and reciprocity issues. They can overdo their navigating tendencies and become gossips, or become overly concerned with how others perceive them. They may tell people what they think they want to hear, or seem like snobs who look down on those who don't meet their criteria for inclusion in the group.

Transmitting: Those with a dominant bias toward Transmitting tend to focus on demonstrating their charm, charisma, and accomplishments. They are both broad-casters and narrow-casters. They unconsciously transmit signals to attract attention and then home in on those who are receptive to their signals, establishing intense connection with specific individuals, if only for a short period of time. The transmitting instinctual bias also compels them to leave an impression on their world, creating a legacy that ensures that part of them lives on. They can overdo their transmitting tendencies and draw too much attention to themselves, taking up all the "space" in the room and leaving others feeling unimportant and ignored or, conversely, smothered by the transmitter's intensity.

    The first step in working with the instinctual biases is to honor what they do for us. They make it easier for us to survive, interact appropriately with the group, and bond deeply with others. Without them, we would be lost.
    But, given free reign, the biases can also cause suffering. We need to learn to observe our habitual patterns of instinctual focus and behavior, and right ourselves when we start to go off course. We can practice letting go of instinctual impulses when we overdo them or intuit needs that don't really exist. We can learn to incorporate the

behaviors related to the instinctual domains that cause us conflict, or attend to the instinctual needs that we tend to overlook.

As we get better at seeing and managing the instinctual biases in ourselves, we can learn to recognize the same patterns in others, using this recognition to develop more empathy toward others' habitual patterns and different value systems. We can begin to recognize how these patterns affect society and how we can more effectively work toward social change, becoming better stewards of our planet and those who share it with us. •

Joining the Dance of Evolution:

Restoring the Power of Belief and Creativity in the Midst of Conflict and Crisis

By Brie Stoner

"MAMA, MAMA...DANCE PAWTY? Dance pawty pwease???" My three-year-old looked up at me with his impossibly huge eyes, filled with playful expectation. We've gotten in this habit of dancing almost every day, letting the rhythm of music carry us into shaking off some of the day's charge.

As I've considered our little dance tradition, it strikes me that there is something inherently evolutionary about it: Like music, evolution does not invite us to "identify" with any one particular posture, but instead beckons us to *keep moving with it*. Evolution invites us to become utterly free from shame or self-consciousness, entrusting ourselves to the music and participating with it, in playfulness, creativity, and the fullness of our incarnate reality.

In this great unfolding symphony of evolution, all of us are participants in the dance of the greater becoming of all things. In *The Phenomenon of Man*, Pierre Teilhard de Chardin outlines the great story of evolution, tracing its creative, groping path from the development of consciousness to our present modern age. As a paleontologist and Jesuit priest, he was able to move past the binary split of spirit vs. matter, instead becoming a visionary mystic who saw the story of evolution and the essence of Divine reality as one and the same unfolding.

The universe is in the process of becoming, and the directional thrust of its formation is—according to Teilhard—from states of disorder into greater states of complexity and union. Today, in the realm of consciousness, or the "noosphere," as he calls it, God-in-evolution's continued work proceeds in *collaboration* with humanity in the midst of our creativity.[1]

This progressive co-creation is hard for us to believe. It goes against the grain of our standard Christian narrative, which places perfection *behind* us in an *ex-nihilo* paradise lost through our sinfulness, despite the scientific collective consensus that now confirms our origins did not commence with a fully formed universe. Far from "fallen," Teilhard describes humanity as quite *worthy* indeed, and our universe's "best" as yet to come.

We often resist the implied, infinite *love of the particular* that this reality would represent, choosing instead to fall hard on more familiar theological lines of God's omnipotence and grace working despite our "fallen ways," and this is certainly the camp in which we are *most* comfortable. After all, identifying ourselves as unworthy allows for lowered expectations and permission to remain a bit more entrenched in our habitual, dualistic thinking, projecting God as somewhere *out there*, apart from us. Let's consider, however, what Teilhard implies, asserting humanity's role in evolution:

All of us are participants in the dance of the greater becoming of all things.

Evolution, by becoming conscious of itself in the depths of ourselves, only needs to look at itself in the mirror to perceive itself in all its depths and to decipher itself. In addition it becomes free to dispose of itself—it can give itself or refuse itself. Not only do we read in our slightest acts the secret of its proceedings; but for an elementary part we hold it in our hands, responsible for its past to its future.[2]

Rather than being an anthropocentric statement, the role of humanity that Teilhard describes is that of mediator and participant in this great potentiality of evolution, capable of wielding it toward its advance or its demise. This cosmic priesthood of humanity fits seamlessly with the Christian mysteries of the Trinitarian *perichoresis,* the mystical Incarnation, and the Eucharist. The act of participating in the Christ mystery is, in this paradigm, the act of becoming unified with the Divine heart and fostering the right conditions for the furthering of evolution. Humanity, by shedding the antiquated ideologies that threaten to keep our potential imprisoned in cages of shame and guilt, is now finally ready to awaken to its full potential. Teilhard believed that our attachment to the Newtonian views of God—placing us as irreconcilable opposites, solved only by adopting a tribal transaction with Jesus becoming the sacrificial blood atonement—continues to cut off our potential at the knees. What is needed is a pliable flexibility that would come from comprehending the Incarnation as *continually happening*—in us. Then the "Kingdom of God," Jesus' favorite way to describe our potential for an evolved consciousness, would indeed be "at hand."

THERE IS A rabbinical approach to the gospel story of Jesus walking on water that interprets Jesus' reproach of Peter in a different way. Instead of "O you of little faith, why did you doubt?" (Matthew 8:26, NIV) being a reference to Peter's doubt in Jesus, some scholars suggest Jesus is referring to *Peter's doubt in himself to be as Jesus was.* His reproach is that Peter ceased to believe he had within himself—as a disciple—the capacity, not just to emulate his rabbi, but to *become like him in every way,* thereby being capable of the same oneness with the Father.

We seem to have entirely forgotten that Peter was not hypnotized into stepping out of the boat! Somehow his will and belief led him to consider himself capable of walking out to meet Jesus when he beckoned him to do so. This interpretation surely aligns itself more with Jesus' words, "Truly I tell you, if you have faith as small as a mustard seed, you can say to this mountain, 'Move from here to there,' and it will move. Nothing will be impossible for you" (Matthew 17:20, NIV).

Belief appears to be the tipping point of all miraculous activity, especially that of our own becoming. Lately, quantum physics seems to be correlating this theory. Physicists in Australia published a recent study in the science journal *Nature Physics* on "the bizarre nature of reality." The article demonstrated that the state of quantum objects is actually dependent on the way they are measured. In this experiment, the helium atom responded as photons do: behaving as a wave or a particle, *depending on how it is measured by the observer*.[3]

If reality is truly as pliable as quantum physics implies, then *how we view reality* seems to be a critical determining factor as to what our reality *can become*. Teilhard describes the helm of human thought as the new frontier of the work of evolution: Our explorations, creativity, expressions, and very lives contribute to the formation of new evolutionary possibilities:

> Let us bow our heads with respect for the anxieties and joys of "trying all and discovering all." The passing wave that we can feel was not formed in ourselves. It comes to us from far away; it set out at the same time as the light from the first stars. It reaches us after creating everything along the way. The spirit of research and conquest is the permanent soul of evolution. And hence, throughout all time, unity of movement.[4]

If God-in-evolution works from within our collaborative participation, then what is most necessary are ready and apt vehicles of channeling absolute creativity in service of more abundance, reality, and life.[5]

This inner work of spiritual preparation—understood in the Christian tradition as engaging the spiritual practices—has all but forgotten the source of its ultimate efficacy in aiding transformation and healing: *belief*. Not belief in dogma or institutions, but belief in our capacity as *human beings* to become the body of Christ by incarnating the Divine heart in *this particular human heart*, in *this particular body*, in *this particular time*.

Belief appears to be the tipping point of all miraculous activity, especially that of our own becoming.

Back before we all became convinced of our unworthiness by Augustinian theology, the early Desert Fathers and Mothers understood that belief was the critical tipping point that would curve all desires into one singular, creative act of the will. According to the *Sayings of the Desert Fathers*, Abba Lot came to Abba Joseph and asked him what else he should do besides following the rules of fasting, prayer, meditation, and purity. As a response, Abba Joseph stood up, lifted his hands to the heavens, and his fingers shone like ten candles as he said: "If you will, you can become all flame."[6] The word that stands out to me in his declaration of our spiritual potential is the indispensable hinge of possibility: "*can.*"

In order to heal the anxiety of our modern age, what is critically needed is a restored belief in humanity's capacity for Divine indwelling, not by insisting we become less human, but by urging each other to become more *fully human*: by fostering more life and increased awareness of the interrelational universe in which we live and play a unique and critical role.

How else could God-in-evolution urge us into the future, if not through the refinement of human ingenuity and creativity, which seems to come to us in moments of inspiration as though from the future itself? How else would the Creator work, if not through the particular constraints of Incarnation in humanity—through our stories, songs, and dreams, all of which fan the flame of our heart's capacity to *believe*, all of which speak of a continuum at work that is greater than our individual lives?

Teilhard uses the word "groping" to describe the paths life has taken on its evolutionary course through history to the present moment. There is something inherently experimental about this word, considering evolution as arranging, again and again, through its ancient path of failures and successes, always searching and moving onward toward more becoming.

I'd like to imagine that Teilhard's use of the phrase "evolutionary groping" could be co-opted into our understanding of the interplay between the Holy Spirit and the act of our will in contemplation. Perhaps what is happening when we consent to the Spirit within, in the present moment, is a release of our myopic identification: We release narratives that keep us imprisoned in *what was* in order to open to the great unknown of what is possible. By aligning ourselves with the Trinitarian flow of *kenosis*—the Divine creativity born from self-emptying—humanity could unleash an entirely new era of ingenuity, capable of solving the very real crises of our time.

We often think of non-duality as some state *apart from our worldly reality*, something we can attain in glimpses within our prayer. But what if non-duality is the doorway, beyond which we stop limiting our own potential and, instead, wield God's generative force in our world? Of what kind of creativity might we be capable as a human family if we could finally accept that there might just be something about *this* particularity and density (and all the conflict and contradiction it represents) that appears to be *necessary* to express the fullness of God in evolution?

Ironically, this is Jesus' vision of potentiality in his descriptions of the Kingdom of God. Yet, over time, we have divorced ourselves from our own inheritance with dogma that instead projects all Divine power of becoming onto Jesus' singular person, rendering ourselves as passive audience members rather than active participants. In her magnum opus, *God's Ecstasy*, Beatrice Bruteau urges us to reclaim our role in the self-creating cosmos:

> In the case of the cosmos, we can say that God as Creator is incarnate as self-creating universe, including self-creating creatures within that universe, such as, for instance, ourselves as human beings. Creativity itself is what is evolving in the cosmos, and we are at the growing edge as the Trinitarian Life Cycle moves from Transcendent to Incarnate to Realized. We are in a position to realize ourselves as incarnate divine creativity.[7]

THE MUSIC OF EVOLUTION is playing, and we ourselves are being asked to join in the dance with our very lives. If it is true that reality is determined by how we view it, then it stands to reason that, even in the midst of all the violence, social injustice, political friction, and uncertainty of our time, humanity is at the cusp of a great opportunity to relinquish its old identifications and once more begin believing in what we *could* be, thereby unleashing a whole new era of possibility. In a time when media outlets perpetuate fear, division, and polarization, this Teilhardian optimism could allow us to become a radical, counter-cultural, and non-anxious presence in the world: a church that *actually upheld* its Christian calling of embodying a love as inclusive and creative as the cosmos itself.

Each one of us is daily being invited to move from the smallness of *"has been"* into the unknown adventure of *"what is not yet,"* releasing our false identification as individuals and beginning to comprehend ourselves as an *interconnected whole*, thereby facilitating our becoming participants in the creative heart of God-in-evolution. This evolutionary instinct unites us to God in the eternal dance of creating life, and life more abundant: a dance, which, as Bruteau declares, is the point of it all.

> What will we do? What are we "supposed to" do? What does God want us to do? Not a good way of putting the question, because it distances God from the world, but the answer I propose is Be! Be creative, be interactive, be agape, give being, unite, be whole, be in every possible way, be new.... God's ecstasy creates the world and the world's ecstasy realizes God. And you are right in the midst of it all.[8] •

Reflections on the Life of Pope Francis:
The Formation of an Evolutionary Thinker

By Sally K. Severino

I AM INTERESTED IN Pope Francis for many reasons, including the similarities and differences in our backgrounds. We both grew up in the same era as first-born members of working-class families. We both have a devotion to St. Thérèse of Lisieux and seek to follow in the footprints of St. Francis of Assisi—he by tending the poor, I by serving as a Felician Associate. He became the first Jesuit pope, the first to take the name of Francis, and is committed to reforming the Church. I became the first woman president of the American College of Psychoanalysts and worked to reform mental health care delivery.

Our differences are profound. He grew up in a close-knit Catholic family. Mine was broken by divorce. His family members were politically astute. Mine were neither politically active nor interested.

Although we both came to our beliefs through interaction with art and interpersonal encounters, Pope Francis then found support in theologians and philosophers whereas I found support in psychiatrists and neuroscientists.

Through our individual journeys we both arrived at a similar vision of human personhood: we are all interconnected and co-creators of each other; the good of one is the good of all and the harm of one is the harm of all. We also hold a similar view of God, as One who is good and merciful. Pope Francis is an evolutionary thinker; I trust I am on the path to becoming one as well.

An evolutionary thinker conceives of the life of faith as an experience of God that is continually developing and unfolding—moving toward new birth. All are invited to cooperate with God's action in the world, bringing it to the fullness of all things. With the hope of forming more people into evolutionary thinkers, let us reflect on the life of Pope Francis and what contributed to his becoming an evolutionary thinker.

EARLY YEARS

Jorge Mario Bergoglio was born into an Italian-immigrant family in Argentina. "The single greatest childhood influence… was his grandmother Rosa, a formidable woman of deep faith and political skill, with whom he spent most of his first five years."[1] She introduced Jorge to the saints, taught him the Rosary, and read to him Alessandro Manzoni's *The Betrothed*. The novel provided many themes that became the intentions for his reforms, including the mercy of God, the virtuousness of ordinary people, and the Church as a battlefield hospital.

His parents took him to Italian movies. *La Strada*, and *Rome, Open City* were his favorites. *La Strada* is Federico Fellini's powerful rumination on love and hate. *Rome, Open City* focuses on the compassionate efforts of women and children to shield resistance workers during the Nazi occupation. Could Jorge's attraction to these movies relate to his experiences in Argentina during that time?

Jorge was ten years old when Juan Perón ascended to the presidency. Although initially identifying with the Church's social teachings, Perón became authoritarian when the Church refused to be bought and ordered dozens of priests arrested. Lessons on embodying love amidst hate must have become part of Jorge's character, forming him as a person willing to love, despite the risks involved.

EARLY ADULTHOOD

When he was almost seventeen, Jorge felt an urge to enter the Basilica of St. Joseph. "On confessing... I felt welcomed by the mercy of God," he later wrote.[2] This experience formed the foundation of his calling to the priesthood.

During training for the priesthood, Bergoglio decided to join the Jesuits. This religious order had laid the foundations of modern Argentina by evangelizing the Guaraní people and forming them into compassionate communities. Their suppression by Pope Clement XIII in 1767 caused deep and lasting wounds, which raised Bergoglio's awareness of unjust systems. Moreover, the Jesuit missionary efforts taught him the value of radical immersion in the lives of the people.

The Second Vatican Council took place during Bergoglio's formation as a Jesuit and became his reference point for reform. The Council redefined the Church as the People of God, an idea that expanded Christian understanding of liberation as freedom both from sin and from sinful social structures that keep the majority of the people poor.

HIS THIRTIES

Bergoglio's Jesuit formation lasted thirteen years. He was ordained a priest in 1969. When Perón died in 1973, his wife, Isabel, accelerated the persecution of dissidents. During the ensuing Dirty War, the right-wing military overthrew the Argentine government and established a dictatorship.

During this time, Bergoglio was the Jesuit Provincial, instituting his first reform—of the Argentine Jesuit province. His grandmother Rosa's concern for the poor, his parents' lessons about embodying love amidst hate, and his dedication to immersion in the lives of the people led Bergoglio to focus on "three key elements: integrating and consolidating people and property, redeploying Jesuits to the periphery, and encouraging vocations while renewing formation. Each objective served... his overall goal of depoliticizing the province and refocusing it on the Jesuits' pastoral mission"[3] of tender care for the neediest.

Bergoglio's lodestones for how to unite people through reform have been two French theologians. Yves Congar, OP, in *True and False Reform in the Church*, delineated four conditions for authentic reform: the primacy of charity and pastoral concerns, truth grasped in communion with the whole church, patience with delays, and renewal through a return to the principle of tradition. Henri de Lubac, SJ, in *Catholicism: Christ and the Common Destiny of Man*, developed the idea of Church as *communion*, which shapes all the individual elements of Catholic faith.

HIS FORTIES

IN DECEMBER 1979, Bergoglio returned to Colegio Máximo, where he had received his licentiate in philosophy. From 1980 to 1986, as rector and professor of theology, he began reforming the Argentine Church through the reorganization of the Jesuits' theology curriculum, including Argentine history and literature. Spirituality remained key and focused on the Spiritual Exercises of Ignatius of Loyola. Most radical was his training of students to care tenderly for "the poor, expressed in manual labor, hands-on pastoral care, and a deep respect for popular culture and values."[4] As an evolutionary thinker, he was endorsing the tenet of bringing all to fullness, even the poor.

The extent of his changes provoked resentment. In the midst of this opprobrium, Bergoglio agreed to take a sabbatical in Germany to study for a doctorate on Romano Guardini. After several months of study, he made a pilgrimage to Augsburg, Germany, where he contemplated a Baroque-era painting called *Maria Knotenlöserin*, or *Mary, Untier of Knots*. The painting touched on his current dilemma. "Obedience was precisely Bergoglio's knot. It is the key vow for Jesuits, and one he strongly believed in.... What obedience did he owe?"[5]

The defining Argentine classic, *El Gaucho Martín Fierro*, was a favorite poem of Bergoglio, who had memorized long passages, including:

I know how they play the game;
they tie everything up and control it:
I'll untie their knots
if it's the last thing I do.⁶

Bergoglio handed Maria Knotenlöserin the knot of his obedience and she untied it. As a result, he abandoned his doctoral research and, with many *Maria Knotenlöserin* prayer cards in hand, returned to Buenos Aires, where he continued to preach the gospel through his merciful actions for the Argentine people: *theología del pueblo*. Bergoglio's sole obedience was now to God.

HIS FIFTIES

In 1990, Bergoglio was sent to the Jesuit Residencia Mayor in Córdoba where, for two years, he said Mass and heard confessions. Being a channel of mercy softened him; the experience of powerlessness brought him more fully into the perspective of the poorest.

Shortly after Bergoglio moved to Córdoba, Cardinal Quarracino encouraged the pope to appoint Bergoglio Auxiliary Bishop of Buenos Aires. In 1997, Quarracino asked the pope to appoint Bergoglio Coadjutor Archbishop of Buenos Aires. When Quarracino died in 1998, Bergoglio became Archbishop.

As Archbishop, Bergoglio's major concern was combatting the use of the Church for political or personal gain. In addition, "he had four major areas he wanted to develop: the poor, politics, education, and dialogue with other Churches and faiths."⁷ The first three areas

> **Lessons on embodying love amidst hate... formed him as a person willing to love, despite the risks involved.**

EVOLUTIONARY THINKING

further developed his earlier concerns; the fourth was new and became an outstanding achievement. Bergoglio built "an impressive network of relationships with Jews and Muslims and evangelical Christians . . . that went far beyond what ordinarily passes for . . . ecumenical dialogue."[8] It was true compassion for all believers.

A favorite spiritual reading for Bergoglio was Archbishop François-Xavier Nguyễn văn Thuân's notes penned on tiny scraps of paper during his nine years of solitary confinement in North Vietnam. Here is a passage I imagine spoke to Bergoglio:

> Having arrived at the mountains of Viñh-Phú, a reeducation camp with two hundred and fifty prisoners...the voice called out to me again: "Choose God and not God's works." I said to myself, "Yes, Lord, you are sending me here to be your love among my brothers, in the midst of hunger, cold, exhausting work, humiliation, injustice. I choose you, your will; I am your missionary here."[9]

HIS SIXTIES

Becoming Cardinal in 2001, Bergoglio consolidated the strong cross-frontier relationships he had formed. For spiritual help he relied on Saint Thérèse of Lisieux, a twentieth-century nun who subverted violence by serenely bearing her imperfections.[10] In her "Little Way of Spiritual Childhood," she showed him how to "live out of love, through love, for love; a love that is not [our] own but God's within [us]."[11]

HIS SEVENTIES

As required when he turned seventy-five years old, Bergoglio submitted his offer of resignation to the pope. His request had not been acted upon when Pope Benedict XVI voluntarily resigned. On February 27, 2013, Bergoglio flew to Rome to join the cardinals gathered there. Not long thereafter, he was elected pope, took the name Francis, and began his third reform, the reform of the Church.

> Pope Francis calls all people to care for mother earth, who is crying for us to acknowledge our culpability for our indifference and abuse.

Almost immediately, in his apostolic exhortation *Evangelii Gaudium*, Pope Francis published his call to the Church and the world to embody the loving mercy of God. As Cardinal Walter Kasper frames Pope Francis' vision of the Church, "The church is, and is supposed to be, the sacrament, that is, the sign and instrument—of God's mercy."[12] *Evangelii Gaudium* expresses evolutionary thinking wherein we all embody and express God's mercy in this world.

In 2015, Pope Francis published his encyclical letter *Laudato Si'*, which applies the traditional and moral teachings of the Church to the social and economic challenges of the present time. Pope Francis calls all people to care for mother earth, who is crying for us to acknowledge our culpability for our indifference and abuse. He proposes an integral ecology—acknowledging that nature is part of us and we are part of nature—as a new paradigm of justice. This expands Pope Francis' evolutionary thinking to injustice that moves beyond the human, to all of creation.

In keeping with his teaching, Pope Francis declared 2016 a Jubilee Year of Mercy. This pinnacle of his evolutionary thinking invites everyone to the heart of ecological conversion, where an examination of conscience considers how God has guided each of us to become co-creators in a world of good. In my life, this led me to willingly take on mental health care reform to help ensure the provision of services to the poorest of the poor.

SUMMATION

Pope Francis was fortunate to be born into a loving family that nurtured him in the Roman Catholic faith and attuned him to political issues in Argentina. The Second Vatican Council expanded his understanding of liberation as freedom from sin and from sinful social structures. Two French theologians became his lodestones for negotiating true reform. Throughout his reform efforts, he cooperated with God's action in the world: his being sent to Córdoba softened him, his appointment as Coadjutor Archbishop and later Cardinal matured him politically, and his being elected Pope allowed him to move the Church toward the fullness of all things.

We may not all be elevated to the heights of Pope Francis. Evolutionary thinkers, however, exist in all walks of life. We are all invited to cooperate with God's evolving action in this world, taking leaders like Pope Francis as our role models. •

Raising a Feminist Son

By Alison Kirkpatrick

IN APRIL OF this year, I read an essay by Courtney Martin, an author, activist, and mother to two daughters. It was called "The Limitless Potential of Men to Transform Manhood."[1] In the essay, she commented that her husband, John, is relieved to be raising daughters. John is definitely male, but not an alpha. He doesn't identify with the masculine stereotypes of yesteryear, so daughters seem like a more comfortable fit. He knows the messages he wants to deliver: Be strong! Be yourself! Transcend your limitations, etc. John's lucky; he married a ringer of a role model—a super-intelligent, strong, independent wife, who wears the pants in the family, just like he does.

Sons? John's not so sure what he would say to them. It's confusing enough to be a young man in today's world, much less raise one. (He's right, by the way; it's much easier to teach someone to step into their power than to temper it.) Being a journalist, Courtney ran a little informal poll in her circle of friends and found plenty of men who felt the same way. *Whew! I've got girls. I know the message I want to convey: empowerment, strength, personal freedom.* I have to say, it's disappointing they don't feel like they could give boys those same messages, but I get why. The implication for a boy, based on historical evidence, is that male strength, freedom, and empowerment come at a cost, usually to everyone else. Patriarchy flourished over the past millennia on the backs of the "other," namely women, the weak, and the poor.

Feminism of the sixties and seventies started down the path of trying to beat men at their own game by being even stronger and more aggressive. (We just have to look at the fashions of the eighties to know it's true.) But many women of my generation disavowed feminism for that very reason. We got sick of trying to "out-alpha" the men, so we quit playing, which has really angered some long-time feminists.

But this isn't a case of young women taking our ball and going home. We didn't quit because we were losing; it's because we woke up to the fact that the game's not worth playing! We never got a say about the game in the first place. We didn't help make the rules. We didn't get to pick the venue or the referee. We didn't get any input on how the points were scored or what determined the winner. The game was handed to us, with men favored at every turn. The second-wave feminists were so determined to get on the field that they were willing to get their teeth kicked in, over and over again, just for the privilege of playing the game. It was undoubtedly a necessary step, but a new generation of feminists is calling bullshit on the whole system. They are sick and tired of having to compete, succeed, and perform on every level: personally, professionally, physically, civically, spiritually, organically, etc., and then face criticism if they don't meet some predetermined cultural standard.

Young women are "leaning in," but not to the patriarchal, winner-take-all game. Even if it means never getting their turn in the big arenas (coincidentally, the ones men built), young feminists—of both genders—are trying to invent a new game, one where everyone can play to their own strengths. Everyone is invited to the conversation, to take leading and supporting roles, to find their niche in a system that honors all of who they are—the masculine and the feminine, the parts of themselves previous generations had to deny when they were locked into the essentialism of their gender at birth. (Essentialism is just a fancy word for the false belief that men are *this* and women are *that*—biologically and entirely, with no exceptions.)

Now, I know that my oversimplification of these concepts might ruffle some feathers, but in broad strokes, I think there is something

> Young feminists—of both genders—are trying to invent a new game, one where everyone can play to their own strengths.

to it. Younger feminists want more parity, but not simply according to the old paradigms. They are expanding the idea of what's fair. Change happens on the margins, so if you want to see more examples of where these types of masculine/feminine boundaries are being pushed, look no further than the young women who flocked to the Bernie Sanders movement over Hillary Clinton's campaign (and the healthy dose of scorn they earned from second-wave feminists like Gloria Steinem and Madeline Albright), or the huge emphasis on the T and the Q in the LGBTQ community. Gender non-binaries are where it's at!

SO WHAT DOES ALL THIS HAVE TO DO WITH RAISING A FEMINIST SON?

AFTER I READ Courtney's article, I sent it to my husband, Tim, who I thought might understand where her husband was coming from. In fact, Tim was really disappointed with John's perspective. In his email back to me (cc'ing my brother-in-law, Nathan, who is raising three girls), he wrote:

> I feel the opposite. I'm happy to raise strong women, but I am grateful to have the opportunity to raise a son that isn't a typical alpha-male. The world needs less of those, so I'm glad I get to play a part in moving things forward rather than backward. But whoever we are raising, I think that we need to raise them with less gender constraints and more humanity.

(Hot damn! Is it any wonder I love that man?)

I just wish Tim's perspective were more common among Courtney's husband and his peers. If any of them eventually have sons, I know they will step up to the plate, but I wish they were more excited about the prospect. We need to change the narrative about parenting. *We can't change our daughters' futures unless we change our sons' as well!* We can't leave our sons in the dark while we lift our daughters into the light. It is going to take the evolution of *both* genders to bring about real gender equality.

But I know Tim and I aren't alone in this belief. In our circle of friends, we know many boys who are being raised to see girls as their equals, and to treat them with the respect due a peer, not a princess. Some of these young men are even willing to be vulnerable, to have conversations with each other about their dreams and disappointments. They are intentional about who they are and how they want to be in the world. Our son, Finn, and his friends give me a lot of hope for the future and so do a couple of other people out there in the wider world.

One of them is Glennon Doyle Melton, author of *Carry On, Warrior* and the newly released *Love Warrior*. Although she lives on the other side of the country from me, I feel as if we are quantumly entangled in some way. I share a lot of her work on Facebook and sometimes link to her essays through my blog, #Signs of Love. About a year ago, she published an essay about her son Chase. I think it's a perfect model for how to raise a feminist son. She wrote:

> When Chase was eight, a woman approached us at the grocery store and said, "What a handsome boy! What do you plan to be when you grow up, young man?" Chase looked at her and said, "I plan to be kind and brave, ma'am." . . .
>
> Chase wants to be a human being who is kind and brave and he is already that. He knows that his "success" does not depend upon whether he lands some job or not. He knows he'll be a success if he continues to practice kindness and courage wherever and with whomever he finds himself. Today he is a kind and brave sixth grader and one day he'll be a kind a brave high schooler and one day maybe he'll be a kind and brave teacher or artist or father or carpenter or friend. His roles will change but his character will remain. He is already who he wants to be. So he can just go about being himself forever. Following his curiosity. One Next Right Thing at a time.[2]

Glennon and her husband, Craig, are not raising their son to play the old-school game of winners and losers. If you are yourself, if you are a person of character, if you are conscious and compassionate, *you win!* This kid is going to be a feminist, but not just because he is growing up in a home with sisters who are his equals and a strong mom. Perhaps most importantly, he has a strong dad, a man who doesn't derive his power from dominance or by diminishing the ideas and gifts of those around him.

THE SECOND EXAMPLE of this movement toward a new feminism is closer to home. Here in San Diego, there is a little church called Sojourn Grace Collective.[3] It was founded two years ago by a couple who pastor together: Colby Martin and Kate Christensen Martin. My family has attended several times and we love what the church is about. But what I love especially is that Kate is on fire for feminism and Colby is on fire for Kate, but for reasons beyond the obvious ones, like her beauty and intelligence. Like Kate, Colby is all about changing the rules of the old-school game, even though, as an educated, straight, white man, he could have won big-time by playing for the patriarchy. He has a book coming out this fall, *Unclobber*, about the full inclusion of the LGBTQ community in the church and society; he writes blog posts about why #BlackLivesMatter and he recently completed a sermon series on Liberation Theology and how it changed everything for him. Kate preached her own liberation sermon on Mother's Day.

But there is one more thing about Kate and Colby that is pretty special. They have four sons! They get to reverse-engineer this whole feminism thing for the next twenty years by lifting up their sons. I want them to write a book about that next. Parents who are wondering how to raise boys in our ever-changing world could probably use it.

We can't leave our sons in the dark while we lift our daughters into the light.

SO, HOW DO YOU RAISE A FEMINIST SON?

I THINK THERE ARE a thousand ways and more, but it has to start with wanting to do so. It has to start with realizing that feminism isn't just about the empowerment of women and girls to be all they can be. It is about the liberation of men and boys from outdated cultural models that force them to be less than who they fully are. We have to free our children from the belief that masculinity is synonymous with material success and stoicism, and that strength and forthrightness are not feminine. We have to honor our children for *all* they are and encourage them to "lean in" to that above all else.

But first, we have to wake up ourselves to the fact that this "war" between the sexes is not a zero-sum game; we are not actually on different sides. We win and lose together. Feminism is the path we need to embrace *for now* to get on the same team, but true liberation for both genders is about so much more. It is about the fullest expression of who we are as individuals and a collective humanity. It will always be a dance between freedom and responsibility, strength and vulnerability, struggle and victory. It's about equality for all and we have to be willing to get into this new game ourselves, showing up humbly and authentically, ready to play. •

What No Bars Can Hold

By Ray Leonardini

On a Monday evening, I pass through nine iron-barred security gates before I get to the chapel. On my way, I'm required to get a safety alarm. If I push it, a dozen specially trained correctional officers will be at my side in less than fifteen seconds. The chapel is rundown and poorly lit, hot in summer, cold in winter. An inmate's eighty-year-old painting of the Last Supper is peeling off the wall behind the altar. Its main claim to fame is the face of Judas, which is, according to legend, the face of the warden in 1935. It's time for centering prayer at Folsom Prison.

It's been my experience that the usual descriptions of prison ministry no longer hold true. When I deal with prisoners, I find myself moving from a ministry of message to one of mutual transformation.

One common notion of ministry suggests that I have something they don't have that I can give them. Yet simple focus on presence rather than delivery of a message elicits a more dynamic experience of the spiritual. This *ministry of presence* is more than teaching in the usual sense. It is an exchange of personal experiences that form the context for heart openings and spiritual conversion. The silence we experience in contemplation, particularly centering prayer, loosens our defenses and brings to the fore our own repressed trauma. This is how change begins.

In traditional terms, we have viewed prison ministry as a "mediating" or "channeling" of grace to those who need it. This model is based on certain assumptions long held by the church, one of which is that grace can be channeled only through a mediator. Usually the mediator is a priest or deacon who dispenses the sacraments, a form of grace and of God's loving presence. The priest or deacon, or one specially commissioned to do the work of mercy, offers this grace to those in need.

But after the Second Vatican Council, our notions of grace-in-the-world have so largely expanded that many now realize that the church is not the exclusive enclave and dispenser of God's presence or largess. "Those who need it" are also not so easily identified. Maybe the incarcerated, those marginalized in every way by society, have their own wellsprings of grace.

My ministry at Folsom Prison is less a "channeling" of anything, particularly grace, than a practice of presence. Put differently, presence can be the true from of "channeling." When I bring up topics for discussion, we create a space that allows for empowerment, particularly in the exchange of personal feelings and sharing of long-held wounds. Because of my association with prisoners—getting to know them as persons, hearing the stories of their lives—I am better able to mirror for them the common themes of their stories.

Their stories always stir me. They trigger my own experiences and give me images or ideas that are useful for inviting discussions of our spiritual journeys. Recently, one long-time member of our centering prayer group (I'll call him Jess) told our group of being confronted—challenged, really—in the mess hall by another inmate, who said that he was "too soft" to be in prison. Jess described the moment-by-moment internal process he went through before saying a word. He said he "went inside" himself (to the inner space we've developed through contemplative prayer) and immediately realized that the real issue at stake was not his being "too soft" but his accuser's insecurity with his own status. In the next nanosecond, he realized

> The silence we experience in contemplation, particularly centering prayer, loosens our defenses and brings to the fore our own repressed trauma.

further that he had the dilemma of responding by increasing the volatility of the moment—or not, thereby proving the accuser's remarks. All this happened in less than five seconds. He decided to try and speak his truth without escalating the conflict. He told his accuser, "I'm not soft, but I know you're worried that you may be. Let me tell you that you don't have to set it up that way."

With this one experience, Jess gave all of us a month's worth of material to discuss (silence, the false self, compassion). This is not uncommon. They trigger me, I prompt them. As they respond, our deeper selves are allowed out of hiding in a relatively safe environment. Since we start each meeting with twenty minutes of silence, a sense of silence lingers during the discussions. We call this space "non-ordinary" space and frequently affirm its importance.

This mutual exchange of experiences on the spiritual journey removes the anxiety I feel in any attempt to act like a theologian or psychotherapist. It took me a year or two to feel adequate to this task. Now I realize I'm not mediating, or ministering, anything to these prisoners in the formal sense. We are ministering to each other.

What I am doing is affirming the *presence* of God in their lives already. This is a basic tenet of contemplative prayer: the Divine is already present. Our consent to this Presence is the beginning of a contemplative life, not the final goal. We usually have no direct experience of the Divine. The essence of the penitentiary philosophy is to remind prisoners of their crime, their guilt, their shame. In this constant, overtly dehumanizing environment, there is no room for the idea that a prisoner may have an inherent claim to their original goodness. In contemplative groups in prisons, we are collectively removing the blocks to the present experience of the presence of God.

I think the idea of "ministry," in prison or otherwise, must be expanded to bring those receiving ministry into full equality with the minister. We are fellow human beings, traveling our spiritual paths, associating with each other, sharing the gifts of our association in the Spirit. In our sharing, we reflect the relational nature of our God.

The perfect model for prison ministry is Jesus' own relationships with the marginalized. His encounter with the Canaanite woman, a member of a dreaded neighboring tribe, was one Jesus instructed his disciples to avoid (Matthew 10:6–7). Her nearly defiant claim to her own experience of God changed Jesus' *entire notion* of his exclusive ministry to "the lost sheep of the house of Israel" (Matthew 15: 21–28; Mark 7:24–30). What was it about her that impacted Jesus in this extraordinary way? It was much more than her persistence. Evidently it opened for Jesus an expansive notion of the ultimate mystery he called Father, and of God's grace and mercy.

We cradle Catholics were raised on the notion that a constitutive part of our faith is based on fulfilling the obligations of the Corporal Works of Mercy outlined in Matthew 25:31–46, where we're told, "I was in prison and you visited me" (25:36). This passage is also the context for understanding why traditionally we view working with the incarcerated as "prison ministry." Unless we understand that we are fellow travelers with prisoners, we can unconsciously use prisoners to meet *our own* religious obligations. After all, we are acting as mediators of God's grace, channeling mercy to these prisoners.

Was Jesus associating with, and being influenced by, the marginalized in his society because he was modeling God's mercy for us? Did he want to teach us how to be present to the poor? I think his association with the powerless in his society is much more than that. His exchange with the Canaanite woman demonstrates this. Since the time of Aquinas, we've not had much room to develop our understanding of the human Jesus and the way he dealt with the powerless. I was taught that, while Jesus was "fully human," in the words of Chalcedon, he also enjoyed the beatific vision and lived with some sort of pre-knowledge—and not by faith, at least not the type of faith that we need. According to these theologians, Jesus didn't have faith in our sense of the word because he didn't need it.

But if Jesus' human faith in the divine mystery was a matter of increasing awareness of the Father's presence in the world, as contemporary theologians now teach, then Jesus must have been inspired with a new understanding of the Divine *by and through* his association with the powerless. From this vantage point, it is the faith *of* Jesus that is critical to see.

I think the recognition of *Presence* that comes from association with the marginalized is what Pope Francis was saying when he spoke directly to prisoners in Philadelphia on September 27, 2015, at the Curran-Fromhold Correctional Facility:

> I am here . . . to share your situation and to make it my own. . . . Jesus comes to meet us. . . . He wants us to keep walking along the paths of life, to realize that we have a mission, and that confinement is not the same thing as exclusion.[1]

IT'S IMPORTANT TO REMEMBER that Jesus did not associate with sinners only once they had repented and became followers, or because he had some esoteric knowledge that they would eventually repent. He seemed to enjoy—maybe even prefer—their company. It makes sense to me that somehow, in a manner known only to God, Jesus' view of the depth and breadth of the Father's reign was clarified and expanded *in and through* Jesus' association with the marginalized.

My experience of associating with the incarcerated confirms this view. Over years of facilitating prayer groups at Folsom Prison, I have discovered that the more I participate in centering prayer with prisoners, the more I recognize the change in my own spirituality. I have watched prisoners, as they themselves testify, re-envision their relationship with God. They have moved from a view of God and themselves that was built on shame and guilt to one of envisioning God as the Father of the Prodigal Son, freely and unconditionally offering love to prisoners. I have watched as they have discovered untapped pools of compassion inside themselves that often become available from the spaciousness of their contemplative practice. This growth of compassion and mercy—usually for rivals, if not enemies, in prison—has surprised them, and me as well.

Not long ago, at our Folsom centering prayer meeting, the prisoners were considering the subtlety of the activities of the True

EVOLUTIONARY THINKING

The more I participate in centering prayer with prisoners, the more I recognize the change in my own spirituality.

Self. One lifer spoke up and shared that, a few nights earlier, while watching television, he had seen Cameron Sterling, the fifteen-year-old son of Alton Sterling, who was killed by police in Baton Rouge, standing by his mother at a press conference while weeping and sobbing uncontrollably. He then shared:

> Here I am in prison, two thousand miles away, serving two life sentences for attempted murder, with swastikas tattooed on my body. As I watched on TV this young African-American man sobbing, I first felt it in my stomach, a kind of dull ache. Then it moved to my throat and I felt my breath stop. Before it even registered in my mind, tears started streaming down my face as I thought, "This poor guy lost his dad." Without my making any kind of decision, I felt enormous compassion for this boy, as if he were my brother. Now, if that's not an authentic experience of my True Self, I don't know what would be!

Not all shared experiences are as dramatic. Usually they start by telling me they have discovered a subtle ability to cut themselves some slack. They have realized, seemingly quite naturally, that they are not the worst person in the world, nor the best. They can feel, ever so softly, that God can indeed love them. They may even be *lovable*.

After a while in this ministry, I felt the earth beneath me shift. The idea of doing "good works" for the disadvantaged now seemed off-point. Now I had to acknowledge that prisoners' reflection of the love of the Father was changing my basic notions of how God works in the world. It was as though prisoners were also teaching me, although they had no idea that this was going on. Before my own eyes, I could see why the marginalized and discarded were truly

God's "favorites." Nor was I then moved to the periphery; we were all experiencing the unbounded generosity of God.

I began to realize that the change in my spirituality came from my *association* with prisoners. As I joined in group sessions, exchanging personal experiences of the spiritual journey, I could almost feel the Divine Presence filling the lives of these forgotten ones. It became not simply a matter of a greater understanding of prisoners, but, as importantly, it became a matter of greater understanding of why God seemed to have a special love for them.

As I was present to prisoners and they to me, I found another way of knowing the paschal mystery. This "knowing" is almost purely intuitive. It is available to us as we *live through* and experience our own Paschal Mystery. This may be true even if we have never heard of Jesus. As some prisoners witness their own suffering and dying from a contemplative viewpoint, they understand, in a new way, the dying and rising of Jesus. This knowledge, gained by sharing the same experiences of Jesus, comes from actually and freely being *present* to the suffering of another person.

We then recognize Jesus, and his life story, for we can only recognize what we have, in some way and some sense, already known. Many prisoners have this knowledge of Jesus because their life is no different from the outcasts of Jesus' time. When they develop a practice of holding still in silence, the full measure of the love of the Father drops like water on their parched tongues. Their spirit is revived, although they (and I) are not specifically aware of how this is happening. They are clear that they want more, as I do also. Somehow together, in our respective incarcerations, we experience the Love that sustains and saves us. ◆

What Really Frightens Us?

By Jonathon Stalls

It was the fourth day and I was an hour's walk on the other side of Delaware. The night before, I was invited into the home of a complete stranger, now a forever friend. Life was changing fast and my capacity to trust was getting wider and wider. As I neared the town of Old Wye Mills, Maryland, I began making calls to local organizations, community centers, and churches, looking for a place to stay. Before I knew it, I was relaxed and napping under a large tree in front of the Old Wye Church, a single-story, gable-roofed building constructed in 1717. The Episcopal priest eventually arrived, invited me in, and started a pot of soup for us both. He carried over the soup as I got up from giving my dog a leg massage. We sat across from one another on the wooden benches at the community table and engaged in good conversation about my journey, the history of Old Wye Mills, and his background. Within a short amount of time, the room felt deeply safe enough to share just about anything. There seemed to be no room at *the table for pretense, reputation, and ego. The priest began sharing, in great detail, about the pain he carries inside. I changed my seating position to face this beautiful, friendly soul. Tears flowed. Grace and calm listening held the air.*

I STARTED MY EIGHT-AND-A-HALF-MONTH walk across the United States on March 1, 2010. It was a 3,030-mile journey of profound growth, connection, simplicity, and authentic transformation, found in moving the way we're built to move—by foot.

My steps were anchored in hospitality offered at the homes and dinner tables of 120 "strangers" from rural, suburban, and urban communities, which included families, partnerships, single mothers, college students, commune dwellers, public officials, professional musicians, police officers—all from different political, religious, racial, sexual, and economic stock.

Days into this journey, my flailing certainty for what I felt was right and wrong changed into a more flexible and floating scale of gray. I was intimately becoming a full-bodied participant in the specifics of what moved around and inside of me. I was becoming viscerally connected to everything. As Rebecca Solnit writes in her book, *Wanderlust: A History of Walking,* "On foot everything stays connected, for while walking one occupies the spaces between those interiors in the same way one occupies those interiors. One lives in the whole world rather than in interiors built up against it."[1]

As I walked, all forms of certitude started to fall away. It felt like a shedding of young skin. Rules related to measurement, success, transaction, and even comfort became heavy and irrelevant.

IN THE EARLY weeks of the walk, my lingering judgments quickly vanished when the very people with whom I disagreed or didn't understand invited me and my dog into the warmth and intimacy of their homes.

My walls and my ego crashed and burned, over and over.

At the end of absolutely every homestay, I walked away convinced that people, at their core, are good. This "knowing" swirled around my stomach, through the portals of my heart, and eventually into my tired mind. I didn't need a professor, a degree, or the well-articulated and interpreted words between the covers of a book. The rumblings in my body showed me that we share a common journey of wanting to love and be loved; that we want to feel safe, comfortable, and connected; that we want to belong—somewhere.

It became all too clear that when we lash out with agendas formed only in the mind and not in the body or the heart, we're really just afraid.

We're afraid of exposure and of vulnerability.
We're afraid of the unknown.
We're afraid to be wrong.
We're afraid of abandonment.
We're afraid of weakness, of truly trusting, and the fragility of letting go.

W ITHIN DAYS OF setting foot on the Delaware coast in 2010, my deepest definitions of meaning, purpose, and truth began to quickly transform. More than memorized scriptures, agreements between churchgoers, and certain utterings of the mouth, God slowly and deeply became the bark of the tree, the stillness of the pond, and the exchange of smiles between the precious faces I passed on the road. These embodiments of the Great Spirit affirmed a practice of mindfulness. With each patient step, personal fear and insecurity slowly surfaced and began to move with me. I no longer had a reason to hide, replace, numb, avoid, and fight it. The more I just listened, the more I allowed, the more I had mercy, for myself and for everyone with whom I came in contact. In his beautiful book, *The Heart of the Buddha's Teaching*, Thich Nhat Hanh writes,

> When we practice [mindfulness], we are liberated from fear, sorrow, and the fires burning inside of us. When mindfulness embraces our joy, our sadness, and all our other mental formations, sooner or later we will see their deep roots. With every mindful step and every mindful breath, we see the roots of our mental formations. Mindfulness shines its light upon them and helps them to transform.[2]

I can't think of a better way to bring mindfulness practice into our body and into the outside world than through walking, strolling, or rolling at one to three miles an hour. It changes everything. It trains us, both on the inside and the outside, to begin seeing God, the Great Spirit, in ourselves and in others in such foundational ways. This humble posture invites us into the fragile details behind our own breath, the curious creatures high in the trees, and the struggle in being a pedestrian in today's time. Whether it's twenty minutes or four hours, mindful walking can invite new ideas, new ways of seeing, and new ways of understanding with every step.

❧

Imagine our bodies being active stewards of deep mercy, love, and spacious understanding. This isn't soft, passive, and apathetic love; this is the bold, hard, heavy, and vulnerable love that lays down ego and creates space for everyone. How do we create safe and respectful spaces and practices for dialogue and relationship among the people with whom we disagree or don't understand?

When hate is constantly met with hate, we fail, and we face the kind of dualism and division that will only hurt the very people we fight to love and protect. Authentic transformation has to start inside our own walls. Our own inner life needs to be broken open by great love and great suffering in order for us to walk with others, right where they are, and not where we want them to be.

❧

Since 2010, I continue to walk long distances almost every day. Around me, anxious drivers go from one place to the next. They scramble around intersections, honk their horns, and often miss the hundreds of breathing trees, animals, and people in their midst. Big concrete overpasses, strip-mall jungles, and muddy ditches interrupt the common walking experience. I am often the sole pedestrian at stoplights. Eyes from within the idling vehicles stare at the oddity or annoyance of my presence.

While the stares sometimes wear me down, an inner dialogue keeps me grounded. It guides me back toward the eyes of the people through their windshields. When I catch their gaze, it always seems to transcend the stress, the judgment, and the chaos. This simple gaze reminds me that we all carry stories. These spirit-held beings

Imagine our bodies being active stewards of deep mercy, love, and spacious understanding.

share a journey with one another—and with me—as we all try to love ourselves and stay upright in a hard world. I can't write them off. If I write them off, I am writing myself off. In so many ways, I am them and they are me.

※

A COUPLE YEARS BEFORE my walk across the country, when I was in my mid-twenties, my inward journey raged. When people say life is "hell on Earth," I get that. My secrets and self-hatred were consuming me in a distant, boiling inner life, which was locked and controlled—or so I thought. No one, absolutely no one, knew that I was a struggling gay man, living a lie and fighting to love my whole self.

Life broke me open, and I landed in the safety of friends who could sit with me in my pain. There wasn't any fixing, judging, changing, condemning, hating, or blaming. It was love's way of saying, "I'm here and I'm not going anywhere." It saved me. It freed me.

It's important to note that while many of these friends disagree with my sexual orientation and my hope for a healthy same-sex relationship, that didn't get in the way of their loving me and sitting with me. For that period of time, my suffering became their suffering. They modeled grace and safety in ways I only hope to replicate throughout my life.

I started living an honest and open life. I wasn't going to run from God. I wasn't going to be overly defined by labels. I was, however, on a path to deep and unconditional love of my whole self. I was alive. I began walking, confidently and honestly. No more running, hiding, or fighting.

I was beginning to see others, beyond their status, race, sexual orientation, agreements, beliefs, or positions. I was beginning to see them as divine, beautiful, and good.

❧

I HAVE MET THOUSANDS of people while on simple neighborhood strolls or long-distance treks: People who live under bridges, commute to the grocery store, stroll alleyways, or walk hand-in-hand quietly through the park. Some of them even invite me to sip tea on their front porch. No one is a stranger anymore. They are daily conduits for great learning and transformation.

Our exchanges are often without words, but simply a restful gaze, simple smile, or humble wave.

When specifically walking in the outside world, we have no choice but to see and accept the vulnerable and the unknown. Control and certainty become an illusion. It's a big world out there and our own edges meet the edges of nature.

What's really beyond the clouds? What's really going on in the spring soil when bulbs and seeds start to unfold? What's really happening behind these seeming walls of prayer and communion? Who are those people gathering in a circle around a bunch of flowers? What story moves with the woman who struggles to get her baby and stroller to the store across a busy highway? How has the man leaning on the blue truck experienced love?

❧

WITH BOLDNESS AND honesty, I ask: What is it that really frightens us? Is it our political climate? Is it "that side" or "the other," or is it deeper? Might we be able to accept that the very fear we fragile beings carry is the invitation to trust and allow others into the burning house of our own pain and vulnerability, or to trust ourselves to enter into the places of pain and vulnerability inside those with whom we disagree or don't understand?

I fail miserably, time and time again, but I get back up. I keep trusting. I keep walking.

Let's take more walks in our communities so we can be opened and graced by spontaneous encounters.

Let's take more solo walks to invite and trust the depths of our thoughts, emotions, dreams, and challenges.

Let's take walks with those who are different from us (whether politically, religiously, culturally, or because of sexual orientation, age, or income level) to glean understanding and mercy from a posture of being alongside.

"Red or Blue" is destroying us. Religious traditions focused on certainty and control are destroying us. Allowing fear and conditional love to mandate our relationships is destroying us. Can we begin to slowly walk on the often-scary and foggy inward path—to "be alone with [ourselves] and...truly like the company [we] keep in the empty moments," as Oriah Mountain Dreamer says?[3]

Let's take our particulars, our hang-ups, and our greatness into a practice of loving others unconditionally, beyond their actions and positions. If we help hold this great mystery of pain and suffering (with ourselves and others) with grace, forgiveness, and compassion, we will, my dearest friends, change the world—one humble step at a time. •

[R]evolutionary Salvation

By Micky ScottBey Jones

Therefore my beloved, just as you have always obeyed me, not only in my presence, but much more now in my absence, work out your own salvation with fear and trembling; *for it is God who is at work in you, enabling you both to will and to work for his good pleasure.*
—Philippians 2:12–13

WHEN I was about thirteen years old, a friend and I went to youth group at a Southern Baptist Church. You'll have to take my word for this: it was a *textbook* Evangelical Southern Baptist Sunday Night Youth Group. Like a scene from a book called *Having an AWESOME Youth Ministry* (which I'm 95% sure is an actual book for youth pastors), there were teen-friendly foods (translation: junk food); sweaty, silly games; and a quirky, funny, younger-than-the-pastor minister, who gave us a talk at the end of the evening. I only remember what he said at the end of his talk because, for the next five years, it was how nearly every youth group meeting ended: in an offer of salvation I couldn't refuse.

You see, I was the kind of kid who wanted to raise my hand when the pastor asked the congregation to testify, but my mother was the kind of mother with a strong "side-eye" and a love of quiet in her pew. But that night at youth group, I was on my own. I could raise my hand, walk down the aisle, and have my own spiritual experience just for "youth." The offer was given. I listened. I could feel my heart pounding in my chest. The offer was an invitation to come down to the front and make a public confession: to turn away from my sinful thoughts, the desires in my heart, the actions in my life, and ask Jesus to become my personal Lord and Savior—securing an eternity in heaven. I remember that night because I walked down the aisle between folding chairs, knelt down at the altar, and said the magical words that allowed me to claim I had now had a *salvation experience*.

I had grown up going to church on Sundays, but I don't think I had ever heard the offer of God's salvation in such a simple, specific, step-by-step way. I like order. I naturally gravitate toward clear, specific, rational ideas and methods. And this *glory* was like some kind of neatly structured, religious, multi-level marketing (MLM) program: Get saved by saying some spiritual words during an altar call, wear the salvation bracelet (with black, red, white, blue, green, and yellow beads), learn the presentation, and get as many others as you can to take advantage of the salvation opportunity.

Like every good MLM program, there were prizes. There were some genuinely profitable and immediately enjoyable rewards for taking this salvation offer. For me, these were accompanied by a feeling of forgiveness from things I considered sin in my life and, for the first time, I was awakened to an overflowing joy of spiritual focus that I wanted to share with others. I would learn that this joy was part of the relationship with Jesus, part of the salvation package. Just like with any program, there were phrases and lingo to learn: "Christianese," a way of talking about spirituality within the Evangelical tribe. Language, belonging, pathways that promised security and strength, were all gifts that came with the salvation opportunity to which I'd said "YES."

The grand rewards had something to do with crowns and mansions in a Heaven so overflowing with gold that I could walk on it. Bonuses accrued for good behavior and with every person I could "get

There are events, "moments of salvation," that offer opportunities of hope and promise, of change and new life.

saved." There was a method to securing those heavenly rewards, and methods, especially at first, can feel like security, which can feel a lot like love. I learned to define salvation primarily as an individualistic, one-time, transactional process, meant to take me from death (physical and spiritual) to eternal life, with some immediate benefits—like God no longer being repulsed by my "sin-stinky" body—but mostly focused on securing a torture-free, beautiful afterlife that would make up for any and all earthly suffering. At the time, it seemed like a good, sure-fire deal to me.

If I believe in something, I share it. This was no different. Before long, I was telling everyone about Jesus and this step-by-step plan to salvation. I was pretty good at presenting the *plan of salvation* (also called the Romans Road to Salvation[1]) and I wore that bracelet for years—thinking of salvation as just that: *a plan*.

So, for years, salvation was a single event in my life. The change that was expected of me—and that I experienced—was not a continuing process of salvation. Those who changed after accepting salvation had really changed as a result of the one-time act of salvation, not as an ongoing part of it.

However, if we were to wander off the Romans Road into the Luke-Acts text, we would discover that salvation describes anything but a one-time, standalone event. Salvation is peace, forgiveness, walking, sight, survival, physical healing, and being a child of Abraham, among other things. In each story of salvation, both the salvific event and the process surrounding it are embedded in that person's identity and experience: For the one who cannot see, salvation is gaining sight; for the one who desires to walk, salvation is the newfound ability and experience of walking; and for the one who was despised, salvation is belonging.

Salvation is personal and individual; it is experienced through an event and as part of a process. There are events, "moments of salvation," that offer opportunities of hope and promise, of change and new life, both now and in some far-off time we can hardly imagine. These are often grounded in an actual event: a message delivered, the Holy Spirit descending on a person or place, or a healing. It is not a prayer or intellectual decision, or even a spiritual transaction through a special rite or ceremony.

Salvation moments don't always look like an opportunity or feel like they hold the promise of something good, but they are part of a story of growth and change. These moments are salvific because they are often *moments of bravery* that call us into more trust, vulnerability, self-belief, faith, change, development, creativity, self-reflection, and growth. It is *the revolution and the evolution*. These are moments of salvation, not because they exist as one-time events, but because they contribute to a series of events that work out our healing, peace, forgiveness, and very survival.

In this way, salvation itself is a [r]evolutionary process. As someone who once believed that it might be possible to "lose" what I thought was salvation, I've come to know a [r]evolutionary salvation that I continue to experience as major change and deeper unfolding in and through my life. I don't think that can be lost—it just continues because of, and through, life's changes. My thinking continues

> *Moments of bravery...call us into more trust, vulnerability, self-belief, faith, change, development, creativity, self-reflection, and growth.*

to evolve as I increasingly understand how this salvation is being revealed in my own life and in the lives of those I am blessed to share.

One of the few things that remains clear to me about salvation is that the common brick in its path will be decorated with fear and trembling—which can be brought on by joy or pain. It takes just as much courage to fully walk through the joyful times—which we often suppress out of fear of future pain—as it does through the painful times of life. What a revolutionary process it is to fully experience and express moments of joy, large and small. Conversely, many of us are culturally socialized to deny pain and ignore the trembling it causes in our lives. Instead, we sit in a limited emotional state of "safety," which is really just a paralyzing purgatory of numb avoidance. As shame and resilience researcher and expert Brené Brown says, we cannot selectively numb. The choice we face is whether to bravely and authentically keep walking, even when our legs tremble and our heart beats with fear.

REVOLUTIONARY EVENTS and processes bring major fundamental change to the people and systems in which they occur. This fundamental change, awakened by a single event or series of events, is a process, an unfolding, a progression—an evolution. The process of salvation is an evolutionary process of more *shalom*, or peace, in our lives. But *shalom* is not linear. As part of salvation, it is part of the constantly unfolding cycle of life. Yes, there is fear and trembling; yes, there is pain and challenge; but there are also moments that save us, changes that sustain us one more day, and joy that surprises us. Salvation continues. Salvation comes again. Salvation brings a fresh wave of *shalom*.

By more *shalom*, I don't mean a less-troubled, smooth, conflict-free life, nor do I mean we are required to die before we reap rewards like crowns and mansions in Heaven. This is a freedom that cannot be flattened out into a far-off process. This salvation includes the here-and-now.

One of the *Merriam-Webster Dictionary* definitions of evolution is "the process of working out or developing." In Philippians, we are exhorted to "work out" our salvation with fear and trembling. This is an evolutionary process.

The last four years have been an evolutionary process for me, punctuated with revolutionary moments of pain, like with the deaths of Trayvon Martin, Mike Brown, and Sandra Bland. Through these moments and processes, I have come out of a helpless slumber. I have been delivered from some of white supremacy's lies. My evolving understanding of Jesus as an extremist for love and a rabbi for justice has awakened me to the reality that things like justice, freedom, and full bellies are a part of salvation *now*—not just to be experienced after death. I have sensed an urgency that salvation—hope for new life, despite complexities and contradictions—can't wait until some unknown afterlife. Instead, whatever bits of *shalom* can be drawn down to Earth must be beckoned and enjoyed now.

So, with fear and trembling, I embrace this salvation. I continue to work it out. I continue, through fear and trembling, to experience an evolution, a beautiful, trembling revolution. It is my work, and our work: our co-laboring with Christ, our communion with the Creator, our process of working out or developing or evolving.

Evolution is revolution is salvation. •

Evolution Is another Name for Growth

By Richard Rohr

It is always hard for me to understand why some Christians are so threatened by the notion of evolution. Are they not observing everything—or anything? Why this stalwart love of inertness? Perhaps static things appear more controllable? I suspect such resistance largely comes from our ego and our unconscious. I do recognize that there is a very understandable need for stability, security, human centrality, and personal superiority in the human psyche. Without it, we suffer from massive mental and emotional illness, along with much anger and fear, as we have today. This ego-need is so strong that it allows people to ignore or misinterpret what is visible all around them, and even to ignore their own obvious "growing up."

There is not a single discipline today that does not recognize change, development, growth, and some kind of evolving phenomenon: psychology, cultural anthropology, history itself, scientific discoveries building on one another, the history of philosophy, social studies, art, drama, and music, on and on. It was theology that held out the longest. It thought of itself as above the fray, held itself above what seemed like fragmentation. In its search for the Real Absolute, it made one fatal mistake: It imagined that any Absolute had to be static; an "unmoved mover," as Aristotelian philosophy called it; a solid substance, sitting above somewhere.

Yet there is little evidence that this is the God presented in the Judeo-Christian tradition, and even less in the "evolution" of our Christian understanding of God as Trinity, who is clearly much more an active verb than an unchanging noun. But then, this central doctrine of the Trinity had very little effect on practical theology or the ordinary lives of most Christians. We preferred a stable notion of God as an old white man, sitting on a throne—much like the Greek God Zeus ("Deus"), a critical and punitive spectator to a creation that was merely a mechanical clock, ticking away until Doomsday.

Here there was no clear Alpha or Omega point, no meaningful beginning, trajectory, or goal. The universe was simply the fatalistic, ticking time bomb, creating a history "filled with sound and fury and signifying nothing"[1] as Shakespeare would have said, or Armageddon and *Apocalypse Now* as modern fundamentalism concluded. This does not create people of hope or vision. The Judeo-Christian vision of history offered us so much more than that, but we are still in *the early years of its unfolding*! Of that I am convinced. Even the Christ Mystery is still "groaning in one great act of giving birth . . . as we ourselves groan inwardly, waiting for our bodies to be set free" (see Romans 8:22–24). The great St. Paul was so clearly an evolutionary and mystical thinker, but we made him into a cheap moralist and a mere Christian theologian.

To fight evolutionary thinking is, for me, to fight the very core concept of faith, where God alone is steering this mysterious universe, where there is clearly much that is hidden from us and much still before us—and where "eye has not seen, and ear has not heard, and the human heart has not conceived, what God has prepared for those who love him" (see 1 Corinthians 2:9). It makes me think that believers, especially Judeo-Christian believers, should have been the first to understand and promote evolution.

It was the launching of the Hubble telescope in our lifetime which revealed that our universe was still expanding, and soon a major hole

Knowledge builds on itself, is cumulative, and is always moving outward toward ever-greater discovery.

was also revealed in our pattern of thinking. Many began to imagine that, if the biggest frame of all was still unfolding, then maybe that is the actual pattern of everything. The latest evidence clearly shows that this expansion is actually happening at an ever-increasing rate! Not only evolution, but now also super evolution, seem to mirror the ever-accelerated rate of change with each new technological and scientific breakthrough. Now every new piece of software is out-of-date within nine months. It is indeed scary and unsettling. We all surely ask, on some level, "Where is this heading?"

I have no knowledge of where this might be fully or finally heading, but I can see what it has already revealed with great clarity—that knowledge builds on itself, is cumulative, and is always moving outward toward ever-greater discovery. There is no stopping this and no returning to a static notion of reality. People who hide inside such a death-wish will never be able to help create God's future—or their own. Perhaps this is finally an appropriate application of Jesus' problematic line, "Anyone who *has* will be given more...but anyone who has not, will lose what little he has" (see Matthew 25:29). Many capitalists use this line to justify their accumulation of material possessions, but it is only true in the realm of spirit and knowledge, which alone increase and evolve with usage.

Of course, most of the original debate about evolution came out of the question of human emergence, which gained national attention in the US during the famous 1925 Scopes Monkey Trial (The State of Tennessee v. John Thomas Scopes). With typical dualistic thinking, science was simplistically and entirely pitted against religion, and religion against science—and, as always, people took one righteous side or the other, with almost no intelligent clarification of terms, meanings, or purpose. The Bible was put on one side and intelligence on the other, and I am not sure we have ever fully overcome this divide in much of America.

The Scopes Monkey Trial might symbolize the beginning of the culture wars we still suffer today, and with the same naïve presentations of two seeming alternatives—neither well-defined, but simply providing banners and loyalty tests for both groups. To my parents' generation, who were often less educated, this was commonly presented in ordinary conversation as, "Did we come from monkeys or did God create us?" Thus we were given two horns of a false dilemma and we all took sides. Good Christians righteously shouted "GOD!" thinking God needed their support, and scientific-minded people who had a bone to pick with religion shouted "MONKEYS!" And both sides fell into a big pit.

What if God creates things that

In 1925, there was little knowledge of contemplation, and thus few were teaching or even exemplifying non-dual thinking in the Christian world. We missed out on what could have been eighty-five years of fruitful discussion and enlightenment. We had all been trained to argue and be right—both believers and scientists—rather than to dialogue with and understand each other. For most of the last century, the very word evolution was a code word used to expose and condemn enemies and infidels in many Christian circles. It was a false test-case.

A little calm, clear, and thoroughly Biblical thinking could have come up with a Third Force response beyond the two false "alternatives." "What if God creates things that continue to create themselves?" seems like Divine Imagination to me! In such a paradigm, God "turns everything to good by *working together with all things*" (πάντα συνεργεῖ, *panta synergei* in Greek), as Paul says so proudly in Romans 8:28. He goes on to say in verse 29 that "the ones [God] chose so long ago, he intended to become true images of his Son." Using very dynamic words like time, growth, and development throughout this most cosmic of his writings, it seems as if Paul himself, in Romans 8—a whole chapter of dynamic verbs and active participles—is fully enjoying the waterslide of history.

So LET'S SEE if we can be Third Force people ourselves and remember that contemplative practice allows us not to need to fully resolve or perfectly balance a seeming problem; rather, it empowers something much better and more healing. *Third Force thinking humbly agrees to hold the tension* as it slowly waits for more insight, more scholarship from both sides, more prayer, a longer time, a larger or different frame for the question, and always compassion. It is the art form of the patient ones: those who can love with both their mind and their heart, those who do not need to win or be in control, those who do not rush to judgment or need quick closure.

Evolutionary thinking is actually contemplative thinking because it leaves the full field of the future in God's hands and agrees to humbly hold the present with what it only tentatively knows for sure. Evolutionary

continue to create themselves?

thinking agrees to both knowing and not knowing, at the same time.

One of my students recently introduced me to a most peculiar-sounding word from the world of geometry. The word is *asymptote*. Asymptote is defined as a line which is tangent to a curve *ad infinitum*, so that they never fully meet. We used it in our discussion of biblical hermeneutics to recognize that all words, even biblical words, are asymptotic! They help, they direct, they point toward, but no word can ever fully match reality in itself. All words are metaphors. Thus, for Christians, the word became flesh (see John 1:14) and there alone, in concrete moments and situations—which are always tentative—can we know God and rest in a fragile, yet also a very sound, peace. However, humans prefer universal principles and ideas to hold them at what is really a false peace.

I offer this to you as a way of understanding evolutionary thinking. Perhaps the reason we fight or deny it is that all evolutionary thinking is profoundly asymptotic! It does not allow us to rest inside of any self-created final explanations—except a final promise of resurrection. Perhaps the line is God and we are the curve—tending toward God but never, in this world, fully connecting. Evolutionary thinking sends us on a trajectory, where the ride is itself the destination, and the goal is never clearly in sight. *To stay on the ride, to trust the trajectory, to know it is moving, and moving somewhere always better,* is just another way to describe faith. We are all in evolution all the time, it seems to me. It is the best, the truest, way to think. ●

NOTES

Nada Mas
1. Virginia Weir, "Nada Mas," *Course Rind, Sweet Fruit* (Bridgeport: Virginia Weir, 2016).

Negative Space
1. Pope John Paul II, "General Audience," July 21, 1999, http://w2.vatican.va/content/john-paul-ii/en/audiences/1999/documents/hf_jp-ii_aud_21071999.html.

Evolving Wild:
Glimpses of the Garden City
1. Thomas Hobbes, *The Leviathan* (New York: Penguin, 1982).
2. Max King, *The Problem of Time* (Warren, Ohio: Bimillennial Press, 1987), presence.tv/home/wp-content/uploads/2016/02/The-Problem-of-Time-Max-King.pdf.
3. Charles Eisenstein, *The More Beautiful World Our Hearts Know Is Possible (Sacred Activism)* (Berkeley: North Atlantic/Evolver Editions, 2013).

Evidential Medicine for Our Collective Soul
1. Michael Dowd, "The Evidential Reformation: Facts as Scripture, Ecology as Theology," YouTube video, 54:39, May 16, 2016, https://youtu.be/lrkQUGUKa64; and Michael Dowd, "The Evidential Reformation: Humanity Comes of Age," *The Huffington Post*, April 17, 2012, http://www.huffingtonpost.com/rev-michael-dowd/the-evidential-reformation-humanity-comes-of-age_b_1421966.html.
2. David Abram, *The Spell of the Sensuous: Perception and Language in a More-Than-Human World* (New York: Pantheon, 1996).
3. John Michael Greer, "Problems and Predicaments," *The Archdruid Report*, August 31, 2006, http://thearchdruidreport.blogspot.com/2006/08/problems-and-predicaments.html.

4 David Roberts, "Climate Change Is Simple," YouTube video, 15:01, remix of TEDx talk published October 15, 2012, https://youtu.be/pznsPkJy2x8; James Hansen, *Storms of my Grandchildren: The Truth About the Coming Climate Catastrophe and Our Last Chance to Save Humanity* (New York: Bloomsbury USA, 2009); Joseph Romm, *Climate Change: What Everyone Needs to Know* (New York: Oxford University Press, 2015); Skeptical Science: Getting Skeptical About Global Warming Skepticism, http://www.skepticalscience.com.

5 John Englander, *High Tide on Main Street: Rising Sea Level and the Coming Coastal Crisis*, Second Edition (Boca Raton, FL: Science Bookshelf, 2013).

6 John Englander, "Why Sea Level will Rise for Centuries; ultimately 100 feet +," *John Englander* (blog), July 20, 2011, http://johnenglander.net/sea-level-rise-blog/why-sea-level-will-rise-centuries-ultimately-100-feet.

7 Esther Yu-Hsi Lee, "Rio Olympics Opening Ceremony Reminds World That Climate Change is Very Real," *Nation of Change*, August 6, 2016, http://www.nationofchange.org/2016/08/06/rio-olympics-opening-ceremony-reminds-world-climate-change-real/.

8 Richard Heinberg, *Afterburn: Society Beyond Fossil Fuels* (Gabriola Island, BC, Canada: New Society, 2015); The Association for the Study of Peak Oil (ASPO), http://peak-oil.org; Peak Oil Barrel, http://peakoilbarrel.com.

9 Richard Heinberg and David Fridley, *Our Renewable Future: Laying the Path for One Hundred Percent Clean Energy* (Washington, DC: Island Press, 2016).

10 William Ophuls, *Immoderate Greatness: Why Civilizations Fail* (North Charleston, SC: CreateSpace, 2012); Jared Diamond, *Collapse: How Societies Choose to Fail or Succeed* (New York: Viking, 2005); Will & Ariel Durant, *The Lessons of History* (New York: Simon & Shuster, 2012); William R. Catton, Jr., *Overshoot: The Ecological Basis of Revolutionary Change* (Champaign: University of Illinois Press, 1980).

11 David R. Montgomery, *Dirt: The Erosion of Civilizations* (Berkeley: University of California Press, 2012); John Michael Greer, *Dark Age America: Climate Change, Cultural Collapse, and the Hard Future Ahead* (Gabriola Island, BC, Canada: New Society, 2016), 30–38; and John Michael Greer, "Dark Age America: A Bitter Legacy," *The Archdruid Report*, August 13, 2014, http://thearchdruidreport.blogspot.com/2014/08/dark-age-america-bitter-legacy.html.

12 Attributed to Robert Louis Stevenson, https://www.goodreads.com/quotes/6583723-sooner-or-later-we-all-sit-down-to-a-banquet.

13 Elizabeth Kolbert, *The Sixth Extinction: An Unnatural History* (New York: Henry Holt, 2014); Edward O. Wilson, *The Diversity of Life* (Cambridge, MA: Harvard University Press, 2010); and Edward O. Wilson, *The Future of Life* (New York: Vintage, 2003).

14 For more on this idea, see "Assisted Colonization," *Wikipedia*, https://en.wikipedia.org/wiki/Assisted_colonization and "Assisted Migration," http://www.torreyaguardians.org/assisted-migration.html.

15 John Michael Greer, "Cultural Conservers," *Energy Bulletin*, May 21, 2008, http://www2.energybulletin.net/node/44584; Greer, *Dark Age America*, 177–198.

16 "Bill Nye's Global Meltdown: The Five Stages of Climate Change Grief," *National Geographic Explorer*, YouTube video, 43:57, January 28, 2016, https://youtu.be/29Xv_npmS6E; John Michael Greer, *Not the Future We Ordered: Peak Oil, Psychology, and the Myth of Progress* (London: Karnac Books, 2013), 101–120; Joanna Macy and Chris Johnstone, *Active Hope: How to Face the Mess We're in without Going Crazy* (Novato, CA: New World Library, 2012).

17 Loyal Rue, *Everybody's Story: Wising Up to the Epic of Evolution* (Albany: State University of New York Press, 2000).

18 Catton, *Overshoot*; for information on a formula that calculates human impact on the environment, see "I = PAT," *Wikipedia*, https://en.wikipedia.org/wiki/I_%3D_PAT.

19 For more on Grace Limits and Systemic Piety, see http://thegreatstory.org/grace-limits-audios.html.

20 The content of these commandments/rules/guidelines derives from humanity's current best scholarship in religion and science, especially the field of ecology. The wording has been influenced by dozens of friends and colleagues who work at the intersection of science, inspiration, and sustainability. Further suggestions for improvement are most welcome. Email Michael.Dowd@ThankGodforEvolution.com.

21 Michael Dowd, *Thank God for Evolution: How the Marriage of Science and Religion Will Transform Your Life and Our World* (New York: Penguin, 2009), 65–137.

22 Conservation International, "Nature Is Speaking," http://www.conservation.org/nature-is-speaking/Pages/default.aspx.

23 Stuart Guthrie, *Faces in the Clouds: A New Theory of Religion* (New York: Oxford University Press, 1993); Michael Dowd, "God: Personification ≠ Person," *The Huffington Post*, April 10, 2013, http://www.huffingtonpost.com/rev-michael-dowd/god-is-a-personification-_b_2866764.html.

24 A longer, annotated text version, as well as two distinct video versions, can be accessed via http://TenCommandmentsforToday.org.

25 Thomas Berry, *The Great Work: Our Way Into the Future* (New York: Broadway Books, 2009).

Mystic Love, Unbound:
A Reclaimed, Reframed, and Evolving Love Story between God and the World

1 Norman Doidge, *The Brain That Changes Itself: Stories of Personal Triumph from the Frontiers of Brain Science* (New York: Penguin Books, 2007), xvii–xx.

2 HeartMath Institute, "Science of the Heart." https://www.heartmath.org/research/science-of-the-heart/.

3 Marco Iacoboni, *Mirroring People: The Science of Empathy and How We Connect with Others* (New York: Picador, 2009), 4–8.

4 Barbara Holmes, *Joy, Unspeakable: Contemplative Practices of the Black Church* (Minneapolis, MN: Fortress Press, 2004).

Joining the Dance of Evolution:
Restoring the Power of Belief and Creativity in the Midst of Conflict and Crisis

1 Pierre Teilhard de Chardin, *The Phenomenon of Man*, trans. Bernard Wall (New York: Harper & Row, 1959), 220–221.

2 Ibid., 226.

3 Australian National University, "Experiment Confirms Quantum Theory Weirdness," May 27, 2015, http://www.anu.edu.au/news/all-news/experiment-confirms-quantum-theory-weirdness.

4 Ibid.

5 Jesus said, "I have come that you may have life more abundantly" (John 10:10).

6 *The Sayings of the Desert Fathers*, trans. Benedicta Ward (Kalamazoo, MI: Cistercian Publicatons, 1975), 103.

7 Beatrice Bruteau, *God's Ecstasy* (New York: Crossroad, 1997), 178.

8 Ibid., 178–179.

Reflections on the Life of Pope Francis: The Formation of an Evolutionary Thinker

1. Austen Ivereigh, *The Great Reformer: Francis and the Making of a Radical Pope* (New York: Picador, 2015), 13.
2. Pope Francis, *The Name of God is Mercy: A Conversation with Andrea Tornielli*, trans. Oonagh Stransky (New York: Random House, 2016), 11.
3. Ivereigh, *The Great Reformer*, 116.
4. Ibid., 173.
5. Ibid., 199.
6. José Hernández, *The Gaucho Martín Fierro*, trans. Frank G. Carrino, Alberto J. Carlos, and Norman Mangouni (Albany: State University of New York Press, 1872/1974), 49.
7. Ivereigh, *The Great Reformer*, 246.
8. Ibid., 247.
9. François-Xavier Nguyễn văn Thuận, *Five Loaves and Two Fish*, trans. Father John-Peter Pham (Washington, DC: Morley, 2000), 21–22.
10. Sally K. Severino and Nancy K. Morrison, "Maternal Resonance: Origins and Hindrances to Altruism," *Advances in Psychology Research*, Vol. 66, ed. Alexandra M. Columbus (Hauppauge, NY: Nova Science Publishers, 2010), 233–251.
11. Hans Urs von Balthasar, *Two Sisters in the Spirit: Thérèse of Lisieux & Elizabeth of the Trinity* (San Francisco: Ignatius, 1992), 72.
12. Walter Kasper, *Pope Francis' Revolution of Tenderness and Love: Theological and Pastoral Perspectives*, trans. William Madges (New York: Paulist, 2015), 36.

Raising a Feminist Son

1. Courtney E. Martin, "The Limitless Potential of Men to Transform Manhood," *On Being with Krista Tippett*, April 22, 2016, http://www.onbeing.org/blog/courtney-martin-the-limitlessness-potential-of-men-to-transform-manhood/8612.
2. Glennon Doyle Melton, "It's Just as Simple and as Hard as This," *Momastery* (blog), June 1, 2015, http://momastery.com/blog/2015/06/01/simple-hard/.
3. You can learn more about the work of Colby and Kate Martin and their church at http://sojourngrace.com.

What No Bars Can Hold

1. Pope Francis, "Speech to Prisoners at Curran-Fromhold Correctional Facility," September 27, 2015, http://6abc.com/religion/pope-francis-speech-to-prisoners-at-curran-fromhold-correctional-facility/1004577/.

What Really Frightens Us?

1. Rebecca Solnit, *Wanderlust: A History of Walking* (New York: Penguin, 2000), 9.
2. Thich Nhat Hanh, *The Heart of the Buddha's Teaching* (Berkeley: Broadway Books, 1999), 75.
3. Oriah Mountain Dreamer, "The Invitation," *The Invitation* (San Francisco: HarperONE, 1999), http://www.oriahmountaindreamer.com/.

[R]evolutionary Salvation

1. One of the ways Evangelical Christians refer to a fairly standardized, step-by-step way of evangelizing non-Christians is by sharing four or five verses from Romans (and occasionally other Scriptures) and explaining the following: Sin is what separates us from God; the penalty for sin—which we all commit—is death; God loved us so much, He sent Jesus to die and pay that penalty for us as a gift; we must confess that "Jesus is Lord" to accept the gift, and then we will be saved and no longer under condemnation; we show we understand and believe these "truths" by praying what is referred to as the "sinners' prayer," followed by baptism, if possible, as a sign of this belief; and then try not to do the things we understand as sin. Following this formula is the beginning of a relationship with Jesus, which improves our life—at least spiritually—and guarantees eternal, conscious bliss in Heaven instead of eternal, conscious torment in Hell. A further explanation of this version of sharing "The Good News" can be read here: http://christianity.about.com/od/conversion/qt/romansroad.htm.

Evolution Is another Name for Growth

1. William Shakespeare, *Macbeth*, act 5, scene 5.

Center for
Action and
Contemplation

A collision of opposites forms the cross of Christ.
One leads downward preferring the truth of the humble.
The other moves leftward against the grain.
But all are wrapped safely inside a hidden harmony:
One world, God's cosmos, a benevolent universe.